May Day Manifesto 1968

Edited by Raymond Williams

Introduction by Owen Jones

VERSO

London • New York

Published by Verso 2018

© May Day Manifesto Committee

1 3 5 7 9 10 8 6 4 2

Verso
UK: 6 Meard Street, London W1F 0EG
US: 20 Jay Street, Suite 1010, Brooklyn, NY 11201
versobooks.com

Verso is the imprint of New Left Books

ISBN-13: 978-1-78663-627-0
ISBN-13: 978-1-78663-629-4 (UK EBK)
ISBN-13: 978-1-78663-628-7 (US EBK)

British Library Cataloguing in Publication Data
A catalogue record for this book is available from the British Library

Library of Congress Cataloging-in-Publication Data
A catalog record for this book is available from the Library of Congress

Printed and bound by CPI Group (UK) Ltd, Croydon, CR0 4YY

Contents

Contents

Introduction

Owen Jones

It was a time of rebellion, revolution, struggle, occupations, strikes – and of living, breathing hope that the old order was in collapse, and that a new society was possible. Nineteen sixty-eight is perhaps best remembered for *les évenements* of May and June in France: the tidal wave of street demonstrations, factory and university occupations, and barricades. The red flag was hoisted over factories, protestors sang *The Internationale*, and revolutionary slogans adorned posters and banners and were daubed on walls, like: 'Humanity will not be happy until the last capitalist is hanged with the entrails of the last bureaucrat.' With 150 million working days lost to strike action in France's biggest ever industrial upheaval, Paris's police warned of a pre-revolutionary situation, and the French premier, Georges Pompidou, declared on television that those in revolt were bent on 'destroying the nation and the very foundations of our free society'.[1]

In London, fireworks were thrown as thousands of anti–Vietnam War protestors attempted to storm the US Embassy. Across Italy, universities were occupied as the so-called Sessantotto movement challenged a rotten status quo. It proved to foreshadow the 'hot autumn' of the following year as Italian society was convulsed with strikes: sixty million working days were lost to industrial action.[2]

In West Germany, tens of thousands of students and workers demonstrated against the Vietnam War, a right-wing media establishment which whipped up hatred against left-wingers, and the establishment's

---

1 'France Enragee: The Spreading Revolt', *Time*, 24 May 1968.

2 Andrew Glyn, *Capitalism Unleashed: Finance, Globalization, and Welfare*, Oxford University Press, 2006, 4–5.

continuity links with Nazism. In Mexico City, an insurgent student movement was met with sickening government brutality, with hundreds slaughtered by the regime. In Czechoslovakia, the so-called Prague Spring and the attempt to build 'Socialism with a human face' was suppressed by a Warsaw Pact invasion. The United States was convulsed by the struggles of the civil rights movement, the anti-war movement, mass student occupations, and protests led by the increasingly radical Students for a Democratic Society.

That's the context in which this Manifesto should be seen. This was a time of ferment, of growing disillusionment with Keynesian consensus capitalism, Western imperialism, and Stalinist authoritarianism. The British New Left – which finds its definitive political expression in this Manifesto – cannot be divorced from these trends.

Reading the Manifesto today, it is easy to be struck by the similarities and the differences. There is the obvious preoccupation with inequality of wealth and income, as well as poverty: back then, 14 per cent were classed as living in poverty, compared to over a fifth today.[3] Today, most British households below the poverty line are in work. The Manifesto boldly emphasises 'the need for socialist priorities within housing'. Today, the decimation of council housing has left millions languishing on social housing waiting lists or driven into an unregulated, insecure, often extortionate, privately rented sector. Rough sleeping has surged by 169 per cent since the Tories came to power in 2010.[4]

The Manifesto rightly hails the NHS as a 'major attempt ... to establish a new standard of civilized community care', but bemoans 'dilapidated hospitals; bad pay and conditions' as well as 'the draining of the public sector for private medical provision'. Today's NHS has been subject to privatisation and marketisation – under both New Labour and the Tories; the longest squeeze in funding as a proportion of the economy since its foundation; and growing pressures because of the attacks on social care funding. Its nurses are suffering a real-terms pay cut of 12 per cent over a decade while staff shortages and waiting lists represent growing crises.

---

3 May Bulman, 'Fifth of UK population now in poverty amid worst decline for children and pensioners in decades, major report reveals', *Independent*, 4 December 2017.

4 Patrick Butler, 'Rough sleeper numbers in England rise for seventh year running', *Guardian*, 25 January 2018.

Public ownership was supposed to mean 'the substitution of communal co-operation for the divisive forces of competition', declares the Manifesto. And indeed, the privatisation of utilities such as water, energy and rail has been nothing short of a disaster. Rail ticket prices are some of the highest in Europe and overcrowding blights the network, while subsidies are far greater than in the days of British Rail. Water privatisation is such a calamity that even the *Financial Times* considered the case for public ownership, declaring that the sell-off looked like 'little more than an organised rip-off'.[5] And the Manifesto launches an assault on the barbarous US assault on Vietnam. Today, the calamitous US-led wars in Afghanistan, Iraq and Libya have left an unimaginable human cost – hundreds of thousands dead, millions injured and traumatised, millions displaced, trillions of dollars wasted, nations economically ruined – and driven the rise of extremist groups.

Of course, the differences between the age of this Manifesto and our current era are multiple. Stalinism is effectively gone, both as a really existing social system and a coherent mass political force in Western societies. When the Manifesto was written, a social-democratic consensus – a class compromise established in the aftermath of the Second World War – governed Britain and much of the Western world. It was inadequate, often plastering over deep injuries inflicted by capitalism with solutions that could be – and, in due course, were – stripped away. But with its fusion of strong unions, high taxes on the rich, nationalisation of sectors of the economy, and extensive state intervention, it did produce the greatest combination of economic growth and increased living standards in British history.

The current one is no age of prosperity: we are still suffering the devastating economic consequences of a crash caused by an unregulated financial sector. Austerity has inflicted particular misery on low-paid workers, disabled people, and young people, while public services have been shredded. Our governing ideology, today, is neoliberalism, which champions the maximum elimination of the public sphere in favour of market forces, the slashing of taxes on the rich, mass deregulation, and the destruction of collective organising. The consequences have included the imposition on

---

5 Jonathan Ford, 'Water privatisation looks little more than an organised rip-off', *Financial Times*, 10 September 2017.

British workers of the worst squeeze in wages of any OECD country other than Greece, over the longest period since perhaps the eighteenth century.

There is one key similarity between the times. The Manifesto was written at a time of increasing left-wing confidence. As the Manifesto demonstrates, the left was carving out and articulating a coherent alternative to the way society was ordered. Until relatively recently, the contemporary left was fragmented and isolated, and in a defensive position, largely trying to preserve existing gains which were being rolled back. That has changed, and in a manner which would profoundly surprise many of the Manifesto's signatories. The Manifesto was very sceptical about Labour's potential as a vehicle for socialist transformation, casting scorn on the party's much trumpeted status as a coalition, believing it was a 'confidence trick' that merely led to the left's incorporation, taming, and sidelining from power and influence. It is somewhat astonishing, then, that in 2015 – when the Labour left was in its weakest position in the party's history – it took party leadership in the form of Jeremy Corbyn. After eighteen months of internal struggle, the leadership was able to present a manifesto to the British public in the 2017 general election and win 40 per cent of the vote, consolidating its position within the party.

Britain is now in a different political age. The neoliberal consensus has collapsed. It is no longer regarded as an inevitable fact of life. Its champions have been forced to go back to basics, to defend their ideas and ideology, for the first time in a generation. Tory MPs are in a state of private panic, believing that the collapse of their government will usher in the end of Thatcherism and the dawn of a transformative socialist administration, of a sort which perhaps has never governed any Western society. And, just like this Manifesto, now is surely the time for the left to be ambitious in laying the foundations for an entirely new society, rather than tinkering with the bankrupt, decaying social order which currently rules us, which is at war with the aspirations and needs of millions of people. As this Manifesto rightly says, 'only an advanced socialism offers any chance of the recovery of human control'.

In 2017, Corbyn's Labour manifesto fleshed out a radical, inspirational departure from neoliberalism. Taxes would be hiked both on the top 5 per cent of earners and on big business, while a financial transaction tax would be imposed on the City of London, all to invest in services like the NHS and education. A mass council house building programme would be initiated, and the private rented sector would be regulated. Utilities such as rail, energy and water would be brought under public ownership. Workers' rights would be restored, shifting the balance of power towards labour. A statutory living wage would be introduced. Tuition fees would be abolished, ending the saddling of debt on young people for daring to dream of university education.

But this Labour manifesto should be seen as a modest beginning. A wider left should push for these proposals to go further, both before Labour assumes office and after it wins an election. Under pressure from a broad mass movement, Labour should be pushed to radicalise in power – and begin the process of definitively breaking with capitalism.

Take tax: Labour proposes a new income tax rate of 45 per cent for income over £80,000 – that is, the top 5 per cent of earners – and 50 per cent for income above £123,000 – that is, the top 2 per cent of earners. Corporation tax would be steadily hiked from 19 per cent to 26 per cent. But it's important to note that for most of Thatcher's reign, the top rate of tax was 60 per cent, and more prosperous nations – such as Denmark and Sweden – have top rates higher than 50 per cent. Even Labour's increase in corporation tax would leave Britain with the lowest rate of the G7 industrialised nations. There is an overwhelming case, then, to promote even higher levels: to provide the funds to invest in services, transform the economy, and reduce grotesque levels of inequality. That doesn't just mean income. Newly elected Scottish Labour leader Richard Leonard has proposed a wealth tax of 1 per cent for the richest 10 per cent: here is a policy which should surely be extended across Britain.

Then there's the issue of work. Historically, the labour movement and the left campaigned for a shorter working week. It's a cause that needs re-energising. Technological progress could surely be harnessed to increase living standards while reducing working hours. As the 1968 Manifesto puts it: 'In a class society, the majority of men are seen only as a work force, a labour market, and welfare is marginal to that.' Surrendering so much of our lives to working for others robs us of freedom; it is detrimental to our mental and physical wellbeing; it steals from us valuable time which could be with our family and loved ones, or expanding our cultural horizons. Research suggests less working hours can improve productivity, reduce our carbon footprint, free up labour for those workers who are currently underemployed, and make us happier.

Then there is the issue of extending public ownership. The post-war top-down model of nationalisation was actually developed by the right of the party, not least by Herbert Morrison – grandfather of Peter Mandelson, no less. The Labour left – from Tony Benn to Jeremy Corbyn – long professed a different model: democratic public ownership involving workers, service users and consumers. The 1968 Manifesto itself talks about 'redefining the concept of public ownership'. Labour's proposal for public ownership of energy, for example, doesn't involve the creation of a centrally controlled and directed national corporation, but rather local community ownership.

But if this model of public ownership could work for utilities such as energy, rail and water, why not elsewhere? Indeed, Labour has proposed a 'right to own': that is, giving workers the right to buy out their companies. The wider left should surely go on the offensive, making the case for the wider socialisation and democratisation of the British economy.

One precedent is Sweden's so-called Meidner Plan in the 1970s, which planned to compel companies to give shares to wage-earner funds run by trade unions.[6] These funds would gradually become majority shareholders.[7] It is worth noting other examples, too: Singapore is often portrayed, somewhat bizarrely, as a libertarian paradise, even though virtually all land and housing are nationalised. Singapore is an example of state-led development, with state-owned enterprises playing a major role in the economy via holding companies managed by the country's sovereign wealth fund. Such companies are held at arms-length to the state, and are highly efficient. Of course, Singapore is an undemocratic model, but the country illustrates the benefits of public ownership.

In a socialist Britain, such public ownership would be wedded to democratic principles. And then there's a wider debate to be had. Could new technologies be harnessed in the interests of democratically planning

---

6 Robin Blackburn, *Banking on Death: Or, Investing in Life: The history and future of pensions*, Verso Books, 2002, 14–15.

7 Peter Gowan and Mio Tastas Viktorsson, 'Revisiting the Meidner Plan', *Jacobin*, 22 August 2017.

the economy – and avoiding the tragic mistakes of the Soviet totalitarian command economy?

The 1968 New Left Manifesto captured the spirit of the times. It acknowledged the growing appetite for a new social order that would transcend the limitations of Keynesianism, recognise the failures of Stalinism, and oppose the murderous rampages of Western imperialism. Today, a new left must confront our challenges, in the context of crumbling neoliberalism, the self-defeating disaster of austerity, and the calamity of the so-called war on terror.

A radical transformative socialist agenda is not only desirable: it is the only politically viable approach from the left. Europe's centre left first accepted or resigned itself to the central tenets of neoliberalism, and then surrendered to – or even implemented – austerity. The electoral consequences? Disaster.

In the noughties, the Spanish Socialist Workers' Party could expect to get 40 per cent or more of the vote. That collapsed to the twenties following a challenge by the insurgent radical left Podemos party. Greece's Pasok party collapsed from over 40 per cent of the vote in 2009 to around 4 per cent in a matter of years. Germany's Social Democrats under Martin Schulz – once hailed by Labour's right as an example to emulate – amassed just 20 per cent of the vote in 2017, their lowest post-war share. The French Socialist Party won a derisory 6 per cent in the 2017 presidential election, completely eclipsed by the radical candidacy of Jean-Luc Mélenchon. The Dutch Labour Party amassed a quarter of the vote in 2012; five years later, less than 6 per cent. We could go on. In this context, British Labour amassing 40 per cent of the vote seems near-miraculous: another exception being Portugal, where a radical left-backed Socialist government has repealed certain austerity measures.

Without a radical, transformative left project, the nativist, populist, anti-immigration right – headed by Donald Trump – is ready to the fill the vacuum. To coin a phrase, there is no alternative: only a new socialism can answer the injustices and grievances spawned by a decaying social order. As a YouGov poll found in June 2017, 43 per cent of Britons believed a socialist government would make Britain a better place to live; only 36 per cent opted for 'worse place'.[8] From public ownership to progressive taxation, British attitudes have long hardened in favour of a left agenda.

A socialist government is not inevitable, of course. The British Tories represent the most formidable electoral force on earth. They are panic-stricken and in chaos, but a profoundly polarised electorate means that the next election is not yet Labour's for the taking. The vested interests that depend on the decaying status quo, and that invest so much of their money propping up the Tories, are not prepared to watch their ship sink without a fight.

But the lesson of the last few years is surely that only a confident, assertive, radical left that is prepared to go on the offensive can succeed. That is the spirit which runs through the 1968 New Left Manifesto. And its lessons and insights may belong to another era – but we have much to learn from them today.

8 Milan Dinic, 'What if we had a socialist government; Owning a signed copy of Mein Kampf; Fame and personality', YouGov.co.uk, 16 June 2017.

Preface

The original May Day Manifesto was published in 1967. For its publication by Penguin, it has been revised, developed and extended, to about twice its previous length. In this preface, I want to explain, briefly, how and why it was written, and why it is now being offered to a wider public.

In the summer of 1966, a group of socialists met to discuss the possibility of a political intervention. They had no official positions in politics; they were mainly teachers, writers and research workers, the majority from the universities. Nor did they belong to any constituted group, though again a majority of them had been associated, at different times over the previous ten years, with what is usually described as the New Left.

As a result of the meeting, it was decided to publish a manifesto, which was at that stage conceived as a bringing together of existing socialist positions and analysis, as a counter-statement to the Labour government's policies and explanations. Three editors were appointed: Edward Thompson, who had been one of the founders of the *New Reasoner*; Stuart Hall, one of the founders of *Universities and Left Review*; and myself. We began work, but it soon became apparent that, though much useful material existed, it was more than a matter of putting it together; indeed at certain critical points of connexion it had all to be reworked. The original group was extended, through successive drafts, and finally, with money subscribed in small sums by members of the group, the Manifesto was privately published and distributed. The response was so considerable that it had to be reprinted several times, and we were overwhelmed by letters and requests for speakers. From many other countries, also, we received letters and comments, and the Manifesto has been translated, in whole or in part, into several languages.

Political decisions followed from this, and are discussed in this new
version. But also, the necessary process of intellectual work, developing the
Manifesto's analysis, was continued. The group, now considerably enlarged,
set up specialist working groups, and a new editor and editorial committee.
The present version is the result of that extended study and discussion, and
takes into account all the other discussions, in meetings in different parts of
the country, which followed the original publication.

This is the internal history of the Manifesto, and it is worth recording
because the fact of a self-organizing, self-financed socialist intellectual
organization is important: not only against misrepresentation, which is
always probable in politics; but also as a specific kind of achievement.
What has then to be described is its wider dimension.

This Manifesto is, we believe, the first connected and closely argued
statement of socialist views in the very specific and changing Britain and
world of the sixties. As such, it ought obviously to get the widest public
attention and discussion. The original version was described in the *Sunday
Times* as 'certainly the longest, most carefully thought-out statement to
come from the Left for several years', and in *Le Monde* as 'distinguished by
the rigour of the analyses presented, the lucidity of the judgements made
on contemporary Britain, the realism of its proposals'. But for reasons
which will become clear in our actual analysis, acknowledgements of this
kind, which we were not looking for, are very different from what we are
really interested in: the effective introduction, into political argument and
activity in Britain, of a contemporary socialist case.

That is what we meant, originally, by a political intervention: for
though socialism survives, as an idea, and socialist activity goes on, in
different minority areas, it has been a main effect of the existing political,
economic and cultural system that the substance of socialism is continually
bypassed, deflected, or, as in the case of the present Labour government,
reinterpreted until it has lost all meaning. It is not at all a question of
preserving some holy writ or some original sacred doctrine; we are
ourselves very critical of much past socialist analysis, and we believe that
Left institutions, in failing to change, have exposed themselves to
containment or defeat. That was always the sense of the description 'New

Left', but we were more successful, in certain books, journals and essays, in communicating a new current of thought, which has indeed been widely recognized, than in finding the self-sustaining institutions, the widening contacts, the effective confrontation with official politics, which were so urgently needed.

By the publication of this Manifesto - indeed by calling it a manifesto, and making it that kind of challenge - the New Left, which had continued throughout as a movement of writers and thinkers, and which in the early sixties had attempted new local kinds of political organization, was at once reconstituting and changing itself. We have no particular attachment to the name; it is mainly what others have called us, and it has become known: in Britain through certain books and journals; in the United States, where we had contact in the beginning with a newly active generation, through a wide movement. The bearings of what can be called a New Left analysis on political organization in Britain are discussed, in detail in the Manifesto, and need not be anticipated here. But it is worth saying that what we are attempting is not a revival of 'the New Left', considered as some specific organization which it has never really been, but a development of what we are content to call the New Left emphasis, which has continued throughout, in specific work, but which in the present crisis leads necessarily to a different kind of political manifestation.

We present this Manifesto, therefore, not as an internal document, but as a public statement and challenge. It does not complete our work, but begins a new phase. It is intended to have not only theoretical but practical consequences. We expect and shall welcome considerable agreement. At the same time we not only expect opposition, but demand it: this is an argument, right in the open, that has been delayed too long, and that now must take place, with as many people as possible joining in.

All the work that has gone into the Manifesto, all the expenses involved in the original publication, in research and in meetings, have been voluntarily given. The people involved are not looking for political careers, and serve no established interest or party. In the one identity that they have, as intellectual socialists working in universities, technical colleges, schools and research institutions, they find also their purpose: to present, to clarify and to continue the widest kind of political argument; and to accept, in the urgency and seriousness of the present crisis, a responsibility and a commitment to all the actions to which the argument leads. They are experienced already, in many different ways, in the practical work of politics: as active members of existing parties and campaigns. But now they put this first: to bring the theory and the practice together, and so to meet new people and to begin new activity.

Raymond Williams

May Day Manifesto Committee,

11 Fitzroy Square, London, W1

1. May Day

May Day, for many hundreds of years, has been a people's holiday: a celebration of growth on the land. For the last eighty years, coming out of this history, May Day has been an international festival - a demonstration and commitment - of the labour movement.

As we go out on this May Day, and look at our world, we see the familiar priorities of power and money, set over against people. But now with one difference, that the agent of just these priorities, in Britain, is a Labour government. It is a strange paradox, which must be faced and understood.

The immediate paradoxes are startling. While thousands of our people are without homes, while our schools are overcrowded and our health service breaking under prolonged strain, we have watched the wives of Labour ministers, protected by police, launching Polaris nuclear submarines. In a prolonged economic crisis, which has consistently falsified orthodox descriptions and remedies, a Labour government has stuck to old and discredited policies: cutting ordinary people's living standards, and putting the protection of a capitalist economic and financial system before jobs, care and extended education. At City banquets, at the centre of a society that still flaunts private wealth, places are set for Labour ministers to describe the historic objectives of their own party - the defence and advancement of the working people - as selfishness and indiscipline. The limited provisions of the welfare state are called sacred cows, and are cut, in a false equation with a still intolerable military expenditure. More than half a million people are left to stand and wait without jobs, and in this new language are called spare capacity. The new generations are generations of weapons.

This is now the dangerous gap: between name and reality; between vision and power; between our human meanings and the deadening language of a false political system. In an increasingly educated society, in which millions of people are capable of taking part in decisions, in which there is all the experience of a mature labour movement and a political democracy, in which there is a growing and vital confidence in our ability to run our own lives, we are faced with something alien and thwarting: a manipulative politics, often openly aggressive and cynical, which has taken our meanings and changed them, taken our causes and used them; which seems our creation, yet now stands against us, as the agent of the priorities of money and power.

How has this happened? This is the only real question to ask, on this May Day, so that we can find ways of ending the danger and the insult that the political situation in Britain now increasingly represents. The sound of protest is rising again, in many parts of the country, and this is a critical moment. The years of radical campaigning, from Suez through Aldermaston to the early sixties made connexions that still hold, groups that still function. The Labour movement, in the unions and in the constituencies, has worked and struggled with a remarkable resilience. And it seemed, for a time, just a few years ago, that all this effort was coming together, into a new move forward. While the Tory illusion disintegrated, the Labour party, under the new leadership of Harold Wilson, caught up, for a while, the sense of movement, the practical urgency of a change of direction. After the defensive years, we saw the hope and the possibility of a really new start. There was a notable quickening in the Labour party itself, and the new radicals, campaigning for human alternatives to a nuclear strategy, to social poverty and to cultural neglect, came, in majority, to work for a Labour government: never uncritically, but with a measured and seemingly reasonable hope.

After those years of shared effort, we are all, who worked for a Labour government, in a new situation. For the sense of failure - a new kind of failure, in apparent victory - is implacably there, in every part of the Left. Not the crowing over failure; not the temporary irritation; but a deeply concerned and serious recognition of a situation we had none of us wholly understood. The obstacles to progress, once so confidently named for our eager combined assault, may now, for the government, have become a platform. But, however plausible the rationalizations, however ingenious the passing reassurances, hardly anyone is deceived. A definition has failed, and we are looking for new definitions and directions.

At any time, in the history of a people, such a moment is critical. For to recognize failure can be to live with failure: to move, as it would be easy to do, away from politics, and let the game, the sound, go on over our heads. There will always, it is true, be an irreducible nucleus of active resisters: the nonconformists, as has happened so often in Britain, losing their impetus to change the society but digging in, in their own circles, to maintain their positions. This minority is still large in Britain, by comparison with earlier periods: large enough, by any standards, to make certain that a living radicalism is maintained. Yet it seems to many of us, when all the pressures have been weighed, that now is not the moment for this kind of withdrawal. On the contrary, it is now, during the general failure, that it is time for a new, prolonged and connected campaign.

What failed to happen, in the early sixties, was a bringing together, into a general position, of the many kinds of new political and social response and analysis, around which local work had been done and local stands made. The consequence of this failure is now very apparent. While the positions were fragmentary, they could be taken, without real commitment, into the simple rhetoric of a new Britain. Now, as that rhetoric breaks, the fragments are thrown back at us: this issue against that. So a failure in one field - the persistence of poverty - can be referred to another - the economic crisis - and this in turn to another - the military expenditure - and this again to another - our foreign policy - and this back to the economic crisis, in an endless series of references and evasions. And then the character of the general crisis, within which these failures are symptoms, can never be grasped or understood or communicated. What we need is a description of the crisis, as a whole, in which not only the present mistakes and illusions but also the necessary and urgent changes can be intelligently connected.

It is our basic case, in this manifesto, that the separate campaigns in which we have all been active, and the separate issues with which we have all been concerned, run back, in their essence, to a single political system and its alternatives. We believe that the system we now oppose can only survive by a willed separation of issues, and the resulting fragmentation of consciousness. Our own first position is that all the issues - industrial and political, international and domestic, economic and cultural, humanitarian and radical - are deeply connected; that what we oppose is a political, economic and social system; that what we work for is a different whole society. The problems of whole men and women are now habitually relegated to specialized and disparate fields, where the society offers to manage or adjust them by this or that consideration or technique. Against this, we define socialism again as a humanism: a recognition of the social reality of man in all his activities, and of the consequent struggle for the direction of this reality by and for ordinary men and women.

2. Where the analysis starts

Consider first where a political analysis starts. You can start from an election, and what is necessary to win it. But if you do, you have taken as central a particular fact, which then affects or determines all the subsequent analysis. What you are most interested in, and what you want to happen, decides the things you discuss and the way you discuss them. Or you can start, alternatively, from the general condition of a country: its overall record, its total results. You can discuss the condition of Britain as if it were some single thing, to be amended by this percentage or improved by that average. But then the general figure can hide as much as it shows; it can show a national income, but not how it is distributed; or a total production, but not what things are produced. What looks like a neutral analysis has in fact been prejudiced by a political assumption: that we are all in the same situation, and have an equal stake and interest in it. Or again you can start from the state of an alliance, or the defence requirements of a particular region. You go on, in a realistic manner, to weigh political factors, to count friends and enemies and the leanings of neutrals. The argument flows, but you do not always notice that your choice of a starting point is a choice of what you take to be decisively important. If the state of an alliance is where you start, you do not look first at the war in Vietnam, but at the effect of the war on the relations between Britain and the United States. If defence is assumed, against a specified enemy, the first call on your resources is military expenditure, and you discuss what is left over in relation to that. Or again, you can start an analysis from particular personal careers: the prospects of X in his new administration; the developing rivalry between Y and Z; the character factors, in this speech or that television appearance. And what is then supposed to matter, to the majority of men, is how these careers will work out. Policies, then, are an aspect of careers, and are judged accordingly.

We are all familiar with these kinds of analysis. In fact, between them, they dominate orthodox discussion, serious and popular. To be interested in politics is to be interested in these things and in these ways. It is often difficult to see how things might be otherwise, how you could start differently. This is how a particular culture imposes its orthodoxy, in a way before any of the detailed arguments start. You may go on to differ, at this or that point, but if you accept those starting points, there are certain things you can never find time to say, or say reasonably and relevantly. The key to a political analysis is always where it starts.

In our own case we have started from our situation as socialists, in the present contradictions of a Labour government. But we have defined our socialism in a particular way, so as to make our position clear. It is not our first interest to oppose this government, or to make what is usually called a rebel move. We do not start from that perspective, because there are more important things to start from. The contradictions are out in the open, and we draw attention to them. But when we say that a definition has failed, and that we are looking for new definitions and directions, we are not primarily referring to the prospects of the government or the condition of the Labour party. We are asking what it means to live in Britain now, with the familiar political landmarks changing and disappearing, and with an urgent reality that we must try to understand, as particular people in a particular country. We believe we have lived too long under the domination of other starting points, and that the kind of politics which follows from them is destructive and pointless. We think we have to make the break to seeing the world in our own way, and then by analysis and description to offer this way to others, to see how far they can agree with it, how closely it connects with their lives.

Our starting point, then, is where people are living. Not the abstract condition of a party or a government or a country, but the condition of life of the majority of ordinary people. Our first detailed analysis will be of what we are calling the social realities, in day-to-day living: in income and poverty; in social relations at work, in education and in housing. We then move out from that, in a widening analysis and description, until we can see the outlines of what we are calling a world system, of a new international capitalism and a new kind of imperialism, which are at the roots not only of the British economic crisis, but of the world political crisis and the realities and dangers of war. For that is the essential perspective, and only then, with the analysis and description completed, shall we return to the usual starting point: what comes out of that reality, as a political situation.

3. Social realities

We have to start with a paradox, in the real situation. There is now serious, widespread and avoidable poverty in Britain, but in another way of looking at the same country, there is a high standard of living, especially by comparison with the years before the war. In the technical progress of the society, and supported by the long struggles of the unions and other reforming agencies, the post-war Labour government made real changes in the conditions of ordinary life: peace-time full employment; the extension of the social services; the expansion of public ownership. There was then not only a higher standard of living, increasingly apparent as the post-war shortages and reorganization were worked through by the fifties. There was also a substantial gain in the dignity, happiness and security of millions of working people. Conditions before and after the war became a familiar contrast, and an important one. This in its turn was interpreted as a contrast between poverty and affluence.

Full employment, undoubtedly, was a major real factor. If the society had simply got wealthier, in total, but left two or three million people out of work, the change would have been differently understood. But until 1967, the average unemployment rate in the society rarely rose above 2.5 per cent. It is true that in certain regions, and in certain industries and occupations, 'full employment' had a hollow ring. Yet memories of the mass unemployment of the thirties lived on, handed from father to son. With that depression as their reference point, most people were impressed by this particular aspect of a better society.

Moreover, although the serious periodic balance-of-payments crises typical of the post-war era slowed down and even at times stopped the growth of output, they did not cause those absolute declines in output which were so characteristic a feature of the pre-war trade cycle. Average earnings, except during periods of wage restrictions and wage freeze, rose fairly steadily. There was for many people a real prospect of improved living standards; and with the rapid expansion in the employment of married women, multi-earner families became very common.

So there was more money to spend, and also, with an economic system geared to the rapid production of consumer goods, a partial blurring of distinctions in patterns of consumption between social groups. Home ownership became a realizable goal for some working people; cars, washing machines and similar goods (scarcely 'luxuries' in any case especially for the old person or the large family) became more widely available. But these tangible improvements formed the basis of a myth, which Labour intellectuals as much as anyone have helped to create and propagate. It is the myth that the basic problems of the distribution of wealth have been solved, that poverty has effectively ceased to exist or seriously matter, and that we are now comfortably set upon the smooth road to progress and greater equality. It is only ten years since the now President of the Board of Trade was writing:

> The essential fact remains that the rich are distinctly less rich
> and the poor are much less poor. The levelling process is a
> reality even in terms of consumption standards; and Britain has
> an appreciably more equal society after six years of Labour rule
> either than it had before the war or than it would otherwise
> have had.

Even when the hollowness of this argument became exposed by the progressive accumulation of research, a process of accommodation occurred. There was no fundamental reassessment of the analysis. The view that poverty had been brought to an end was still complacently assumed, and is still the official rhetoric of British society. What poverty remained was seen as incidental, a matter of special cases which could be treated in isolation from wider, structural considerations. Inequality was similarly incidental, or alternatively was only of that kind essential for providing necessary incentives to make the economic system operate more effectively.

We reject these views. To move from the rhetoric to the reality is to see that not everyone has in fact shared equally in the benefits of economic growth and full employment: that the gap between rich and poor has not, in fact, grown noticeably less. Two per cent of the British people still own 55 per cent of all private wealth. Ten per cent own 80 per cent. Differences of income are still very wide. When income from property is added to earnings, the top 1 per cent of the British people receive about as much income as the bottom 30 per cent put together. These are the ground-lines of all the other changes.

Our case then is: that there are still gross and intolerable areas of traditional poverty and inequality. Further, that post-war capitalism, even at its most successful, creates and ratifies new kinds of poverty. That the policies of the current Labour government, far from tackling these problems at their source, have intensified them. And that it is possible, by a socialist analysis and programme, to reveal and to change those mechanisms inherent in British capitalist society which create the poverty and inequality which, with a shift of emphasis, have now plainly to be seen.

4. Poverty today

The continuing personal poverty in our society is not incidental; it is a matter of conscious social policy, and of the structures of society itself. Poverty not only remains substantial, but the prospect of the comprehensive legislative programme which could abolish it, at one stage promised, recedes with every turn of the economic crisis. Nor is it a question of ignorance. The scale of the problem of poverty is officially admitted, and much of the most important recent evidence comes from the government's own surveys.

The numbers subject to poverty, by any reasonable definitions, are very large indeed. Using the standard of 40 per cent above basic National Assistance rates, in 1964, Peter Townsend estimated that three million members of families whose head was in full-time work, two and a half million persons of pensionable age, three quarters of a million fatherless families, three quarters of a million chronic sick or disabled and over half a million families of unemployed fathers were in poverty. This amounts to about 14 per cent of the population. By basic National Assistance standards, about a third of those groups were in acute poverty.

It has long been known that old age is accompanied by a descent into poverty for a large proportion of old people. The government's *Circumstances of Retirement Pensioners* report in 1966 estimated that three quarters of a million old people lived below National Assistance level. Supplementary Pensions legislation has somewhat improved this position. But if one takes Supplementary Benefit levels as a new minimal definition of subsistence, since 1966, one still finds 1,670,000 old people in poverty; one must add to this figure 20 per cent or more dependants of these pensioners, and an unknown but significant number who would be entitled to Supplementary Benefit but do not receive it. About a third of old people,

from official evidence, cannot live without special supplementation of their
income to subsistence level.

Widespread poverty is not confined to retired people, and there has
been growing attention in recent years to the problem of poverty among
wage earners and families. The Ministry of Social Security estimated that
280,000 families with two or more children lived, before November 1966,
at or below National Assistance level. This included 910,000 children. By
the newer Supplementary Benefit standards (amounting to 14s per week
extra for a family with three children) there were 345,000 families in
poverty, including 125,000 in full-time work, and 1,110,000 children.
One-child families were excluded from this *Circumstances of Families* report,
but if one adds them the Ministry estimates that out of a total of seven
million families, approaching half a million, with up to one and a quarter
million children, were in poverty.

These families in poverty include a large proportion of the chronic
sick, the unemployed, and fatherless families. A third of families whose
wage earner was sick or unemployed were receiving National Assistance, in
1966, while a quarter were entitled to but not receiving it. Though large
families are only a small minority of the total in poverty, nevertheless one in
five of them with six or more children were in poverty by the still stringent
Supplementary Benefit standards. Most families made fatherless by
widowhood or separation had total incomes near to National Assistance
level in 1966; half received National Assistance. Of the half million families
the Ministry estimated to be in poverty 145,000 were fatherless. The
wage-stop is an additional factor, keeping another 30,000 families in
poverty by these standards. This regulation restricts the Supplementary
Benefit payable to the sick and unemployed, where payment of the full rate
would increase a man's income. By this rule, a family whose needs by the
Supplementary Benefit scale amount to £15-20 a week can quite easily only
get £10-12. The law thus confirms the below-subsistence incomes of men
in work.

On top of the wage-stop, there are 140,000 families who could not be
raised to Supplementary Benefit levels because they are in work. One recent
survey which excluded some low-paid occupations such as agriculture,

retail distribution, and catering, estimated that the earnings of nearly 16 per cent of men were below £15 per week. Of course women's earnings are much lower than this. In a number of industries, notably public employment and textiles of those investigated, more than 10 per cent of men earned less than £12 per week. The structure of incomes and employment is as important as the meanness of welfare provisions in the creation and perpetuation of poverty.

It should be stated clearly that these estimates are made by using conventional measures, and are in no case running ahead of what public opinion views as subsistence. A recent survey showed that the great majority of a national random sample of adults described a family with two children as needy if its income was £12 a week. Twelve pounds per week is what such a family would get on the Supplementary Benefit scale. In eleven months in 1967, 372,000 lump-sum payments for 'exceptional needs' were made on top of Supplementary Benefit payments, which indicates the extent to which the government is forced to recognize the inadequacy of its own subsistence standards.

Moreover, although it is true that poverty has been pushed away from the daily experience of a majority of working people, it is also true that it has been removed to only a short distance - the distance of a few weekly pay packets. What distinguishes the poor from the rest of the working-class population is only, after all, a particular misfortune - illness or unemployment - or a customary phase of life - parenthood of young children, retirement. The population experiencing poverty is not static: most people grow old; many people in the next few years will be ill, will lose their jobs, or be widowed. Poverty is thus a condition to be anticipated by a much larger proportion of people than those who are poor at any one time, at some stage of their lives. Poverty is thus not merely a problem of special groups, or of other people, but an atmosphere in which large numbers of people live their lives, and which threatens at any time to assume a more concrete presence.

There are signs of a structural *increase* in the proportion of the population subject to poverty, in spite of the persistent myth that poverty is disappearing. There has been a disproportionate increase in the numbers of very old and very young people in the population. The Registrar-General's estimates suggest that in the next decade the number of children under 15 and persons of pensionable age will increase by 15 or 16 per cent, but the population aged 15 to 59 will increase by only 2 per cent. The value of important social benefits has fallen; Family Allowances are worth less in relation to real earnings than when they were first introduced in 1946. Welfare payments are still based on calculations of minimal subsistence, reluctantly raised to keep up, barely, with rising income levels, while tax reliefs and private insurance are in generous relation to earning for the better-off. High levels of 'permanent' unemployment, the displacement of skills, and a flagging demand for unskilled workers threaten to increase the proportion of workers thrown into poverty.

The poor are ill-organized, and their weakness is exploited. They are subject to humiliating treatment, for example at the hands of the Supplementary Benefits Commission who have discretionary powers to withhold benefits from sick or unemployed men, or fatherless families, without giving grounds. What are in fact legal rights are surrounded by a taint of charity and suspicion, denying self-respect, and so many rights go unclaimed. Nearly half the children entitled to free school meals pay for them. Very few families with fathers in full-time work are receiving free welfare milk, though 90,000 children are apparently eligible. A small proportion of poor families entitled to rent rebates receive them, and only a small proportion of private tenants who could expect reductions in rents from Rent Tribunals and Rent officers in fact apply to them. The machinery of the welfare system depends for its 'efficiency' on the fact that so many of those in the greatest need do not use it.

In part this is a matter of indifference, ignorance and a lack of political commitment to changing the priorities which perpetuate this situation. But the existence of poverty is more profoundly rooted in our society even than this. The poor, with the crucial conception of a 'minimum level', are preserved as the floor from which the competitive ladder can be raised. They still exist 'to encourage the others', as a negative definition of failure against which the more fortunate can measure their success. Modern capitalist society, in generating such tension between desire and opportunity, expectation and fulfilment, creates and confirms this poverty as its own standards are raised.

We believe that a new definition of poverty, and of its connexions to fundamental social and political realities, needs urgently to be established. Because of conventional 'minimal' interpretations of what poverty actually is, the extent of deprivation is seriously underestimated: poverty has not lessened, relative to the common standard of life, for it is the felt absence of a standard of comfort and opportunity which is present in the society, but which is always beyond personal grasp. It can be ended only when the right is recognizable for all to share a rising standard of life, security and relationships in common.

5. The facts of inequality

But problems of poverty, in this primary sense, are only one aspect of the more fundamental problem of inequality. How much inequality in the command over resources are we prepared to tolerate? The myth that poverty has been effectively abolished in Britain is closely connected with the assumption that an 'affluent society' has cancelled serious inequalities.

The 'affluent society' in Britain was made possible by the successful management of post-war recovery. Yet as the affluence matured, it became obvious that still, underneath, there were radical inequalities of wealth and opportunity, and a starvation of the public sector to supply the demands of private consumption. In the 'affluent society', universal public services have not automatically conferred equality of access. More middle-class than working-class children gain university degrees at state expense. Seventy-nine per cent of schools in slum areas are gravely inadequate. National Health lists and school classes are larger in working-class areas. The poorest people seem not to qualify for subsidized council housing, or are obliged to leave it for far worse and usually more costly privately-rented housing.

The 'affluent society' has not, in fact, abolished fundamental inequalities in the structure of British society, and it is to this fact that the problem of poverty must be related. Affluence left the distribution of income and the ownership of property relatively untouched. It is unfashionable to begin a discussion of equality with references to the ownership of property. But this, after all, is the basic characteristic of capitalism, and wealth is still distributed fantastically unequally in British society. There may have been some trend towards a more equal distribution compared with pre-war, but problems of measurement are great. It has been said very aptly that 90 per cent of the population only have wealth when they die. That is when the life insurance policy becomes payable, or the owner-occupied house can be sold. This is wealth of a totally different character from that which can be disposed of by the top ten per cent of the population who own 80 per cent of all private property. Ownership of capital of this kind confers immense power, freeing the individual from the hazards of life which most ordinary people face: how to deal with the unexpected drop in income from sickness or change of work or unemployment. It also gives power to exploit the characteristics and chances of the capitalist system. To him that hath shall verily be given. In a managed capitalism which achieves some growth, and with rising price levels, capital gains become as important a source of increased purchasing power as income itself. And behind this concentration of private wealth lies the concentration of wealth in the hands of the large corporations, the investment trusts and the insurance companies.

As for the distribution of income, it is now clear that any trend towards greater equality was almost certainly temporary. The higher post-war levels of employment were reflected in such trends in income distribution in most capitalist countries. There was nothing particularly remarkable about Britain. The share of income after tax of top income-receivers in this country has remained very stable over the last few years. More significantly, the poorest of the population, the bottom 30 per cent in the income scale, have actually been receiving a declining proportion of total income. This poorest 30 per cent receive only 12 per cent of total income after tax. By comparison, the top $1\frac{1}{2}$ per cent receive, even after tax, 7 per cent of the total.

These inequalities are underlined by other comparisons. In 1913 and 1914 the unskilled worker received approximately 19 per cent of the average earnings of 'higher' professional workers, and in 1960 26 per cent. In 1913 and 1914 he earned 31 per cent of the average income of managers, but in 1960 only 29 per cent. In 1938, the ratio of gross profits to all employment incomes (including directors' salaries) was 1 to 4.5; in 1962 it was 1 to 4.8. Perhaps one of the most striking facts of all is that when we turn to examine the effect of government measures via taxation, direct and indirect, and the provision of benefits in cash and kind, we find, as one authority recently expressed it, that 'there appears to have been little increase in the amount of vertical redistribution [i.e. from rich to poor] between 1937 and 1959'. There is little reason to suppose that the picture has changed since then, except for the worse.

In Britain today, the odds against a manual worker's son achieving professional status, by comparison with the son of an established business or professional man, are very much as they were at the beginning of the century. In the distribution of educational opportunity, the social status of the child's father remains the single most important determinant of success. In the 1950s only $\frac{1}{2}$ per cent of the children of unskilled and semi-skilled manual workers were reaching university, about the same proportion as in the late 1930s and the 1940s. About $14\frac{1}{2}$ per cent of the children of professional, managerial and intermediate occupational groups were doing so, compared with 4 per cent in the 1930s. In recent years, one in every four of the middle-class children entering a grammar school course at the age of 11 have eventually gone on to university, but only one in every fifteen to twenty of the children of unskilled manual workers entering such a course have done so. Upper-middle-class children obtain three times as many selective school places as the children of unskilled manual workers, more than twice as many as skilled manual workers' children, and one and a half times as many as lower-middle-class children. This, as many studies have shown, is not because of some built-in and absolute relation between class and ability, but because of an effective and damaging relation between class and opportunity.

Underlying these general inequalities, there is a gross and continuing inequality between men and women: in rates of pay, most obviously, but also in legal status and educational opportunity, and in many aspects of the administration of social security. Like other inequalities, this is no more tolerable because it has become familiar and is rationalized as 'the way things are'.

6. Social poverty

Poverty and inequality are then inherent in the present structures of British society. This is again clear if we look at those areas which most immediately affect the quality and substance of social life. The whole field of social welfare is one example. The Labour government can point to the increases in National Insurance benefits in 1965 and 1967, but these have already been largely eroded by price increases. National Assistance is now called Supplementary Benefit, but there has been no new look at the whole concept of 'subsistence', no search for a different conception of standards, in terms of what a decent society would give to its members rather than in terms of the minimum which can be safely got away with. There have been some changes in the regulations which allow people to qualify for Supplementary Benefits, but in other areas, as in the case of discretionary additions to basic benefit rates for the purpose of meeting special needs, there may well now be less flexibility.

It was the Labour government which published the report about poverty among families with children; yet the measures it produced to deal with this problem were ludicrously inadequate. Once again, increases in Family Allowance have been virtually wiped out both by the decision to increase the price of school meals and welfare milk and by the general increases in prices, particularly following devaluation. The Prime Minister had the effrontery at Scarborough to dwell upon the increases in social expenditure under the Labour government as an 'achievement'. Overall in four years under the Tories, social expenditures increased by 43 per cent, prices by 11 per cent; under four years of Labour social expenditures increased by 45 per cent, prices by 15 per cent. Much of even this social increase is accounted for by the growth of the number of people qualifying for benefits: more children to educate, more old people to provide pensions for, and so on. It does not represent an improvement in the standard of the services provided.

That this was taken for granted was underlined already even in the National Plan, when it was still hoped that a growth rate of 4 per cent would be achieved. It was also in the National Plan that the criteria for choosing items on which expenditure was to be concentrated were clearly spelled out. The criterion was to be not social need but 'contribution to economic growth'. We have also had clear statements from government spokesmen like Gordon Walker:

> In a democracy, it is very difficult to reduce private affluence. ...
> All one can reasonably do is to take a larger share of any
> increase from them. ... Those who advocate that we should
> simply take more and more money, whatever is happening to
> the economy, aren't on the whole people who have to win votes
> and stay in office and try to get things done. Large increases in
> expenditure on the social services are just not possible unless
> economic growth is going happily forward.

This is a clear statement of acceptance of the values of capitalism. A clear statement, also, of an unpleasant and right-wing kind of political calculation: stay in office to get what things done? For it is wholly unrealistic as a solution of social problems. We have only to look at the United States, with a per capita income twice as high as in this country, to see that economic growth in no way automatically solves any of these difficulties. We need a clear identification of the mechanisms which in capitalist society generate this inequality which we so bitterly oppose. The problem must be tackled at its roots, and these are fundamentally in the ownership and control of the economic system. But there are certain mechanisms which relate specifically to the social services.

The first is the extent to which poverty as we have described it is the experience of relatively isolated groups. The poor do exist in 'pockets' (just as there are once again emerging pockets of rickets in Glasgow and among immigrant children). It is significant that the one group who command most popular support in their need for more money are the old. Many people do have experience of the poverty of old age through their experiences of their parents. Far fewer have experience of the poverty of the long-term sick, the fatherless family, or of the unemployed or the low wage earner. Even among the employed there is not a common shared experience of low wages; particular groups of men with particular types of employer, in particular industries, or with particular backgrounds of ill health are the ones who suffer most. This presents an exceptionally difficult task for the trade unions to tackle, and this is the real importance of proposals for a national minimum wage. It is difficult for the poor in these situations to generate, on their own, any effective political pressure.

Then there is the failure to make any attempt to use the tax system to influence the distribution of wealth and income. Without a radical and far-reaching attack on the distribution of private property through a wealth tax, very little progress can be made. But even marginal progress is unlikely while the government insists upon viewing taxes and social benefits as virtually separate systems (except when it comes to paying increased National Insurance benefits when it is always thought legitimate to increase one of the most reactionary taxes of all, the National Insurance contribution).

The third mechanism of inequality is the acceptance of a continued and ever growing private sector in direct competition with the public sector in the provision of social services. The 'public' schools are the most obvious example. But such competition exists too in the field of sickness benefits, occupational pensions and, not least, the health service. The private sector, untrammelled by limitations put upon the public spending, can bid far more effectively for resources. It can then not only supply higher standards, giving advantage to those who have the money to pay; it also succeeds in a growing number of cases in giving the public service the flavour of a second-class service.

Social realities and social values interact. It is under the Labour government, and with its connivance, that the attack on the basic principle of the 'free' social services has reached its peak. Once again the battle cry is 'only to those who need it', and the terms 'universality' versus 'selectivity' are bandied about. Alternatively the cry goes up 'to each according to his ability to pay'. Despite some elements of redistribution contained within it, this is the fundamental principle of the Labour party's own superannuation plan for wage-related pensions. The government has made an attempt to beat the market at its own game (i.e. private occupational pensions). But without control the market proves too strong.

In isolation from a general strategy for moving towards greater equality, the debate about 'universality' and 'selectivity' is meaningless. 'Selectivity' may be a useful way of rationing scarce resources; or it may be a way of stigmatizing second-class citizens. It depends on the context, on what other things are happening. And the other things that are now actually happening, in a whole social and economic policy, are in the interest of a persistent inequality.

7. Housing, health and education

Housing

The failure to make housing a social service and to break the speculative and bureaucratic interests which still stand between people and decent homes continues to outrage conscience.

It is not only the heartbreaking problem of the homeless. It is also the failure to prevent rents rising; to challenge what items can properly be included in a housing account which is all too glibly said to be in deficit; to stop the Tories selling off the social property of council housing. Again, the persistent ugliness of our cities brought a notable response from architects and planners, who have shown repeatedly, given the least chance, how a civilized modern environment can be created. But it is not only that they have to live, like the rest of us, in the shadow of a financial policy which, pushing up interest rates, has made the moneylenders the only effective planners. It is also that when the conflict comes, as it seems to come in every city and town, between community needs and established or speculative commercial interests, there is a scandalous absence of any real national lead, any public dramatization of the essential conflict, with all the facts in the open, so that we could fight the issue right through. Commercial and financial priorities have been learned too well, and many people are tired of fighting them. The weak and needy, without resources, have to put up with what they can get, at a still scandalous market price. Labour's attempts to assert a different policy have been slow and feeble; they have come from one part of the split mind of the party, its residual social objectives, and have been unable to prevail against the commercial run of the society which is elsewhere being actively protected and encouraged. No social policy can be carried through in isolation. All that happens, as now in housing, is that it declines to a marginal need.

When Labour came to power, it announced the need for the immediate reimposition of rent control and the acceleration of the building programme to an ultimate target of 500,000 houses a year. Its housing programme since 1964 has in fact suffered continually from the lack of any planned and consistent perspective, revealing at every point timidity, fragmentation and compromise.

One obvious field in which these qualities have dominated is that of subsidies to owner-occupiers and local authority tenants. It is preposterous that a Labour government is urging local authorities to charge its better-off tenants economic rents *before* abolishing the tax-relief subsidy for owner-occupiers, which increases as the owner-occupier becomes more wealthy and can afford a more expensive home. The mortgage option scheme, in this context, can be nothing more than a sop to socialist conscience; it is a curious kind of 'socialist' government which prides itself on giving for the first time to the poorer owner-occupiers some of the advantages which still accrue to the richer owner-occupiers. It will still remain the case that the subsidy for owner-occupiers will increase with their income.

The problem of high rents and insecurity of tenure, before the 1965 Rent Act, was overwhelmingly a problem of the 'twilight' areas of the large cities - Sparkbrook, Notting Hill and similar districts. Yet the form of the Rent Act, demanding as it does both knowledge and initiative from the tenant, is least appropriate for the immigrants, migrants, old people and social outcasts who largely compose the population of these districts. In order to 'take rents out of politics', by setting up a structure which involves 'agreements' on 'fair rents' between landlord and tenant, rather than the simple and rigid rent control related to rateable value which existed before 1957, the government has sacrificed many of those most in need of protection. Even where the tenant knows the Act (and there is evidence of widespread ignorance) the structure is weighted against him. There has been evidence of landlords offering revised rents which remain far above what a Rent Officer would consider suitable, and which the tenant gratefully accepts. There have been cases of new tenancies refused to people who show signs of familiarity with the Act. There is no legal aid available for tenants who appear before rent tribunals. Unlike his landlord, the tenant has no body of case-law which can aid him in his interpretation of what constitutes a fair rent.

In the field of subsidies for local authority building, the projected fifty-fifty spread between the public and private housing sectors will lead only to a continued misallocation of funds, unless the government confronts the need for price controls in the private sector. Mortgage option schemes, tax relief on the interest of mortgage repayments, subsidies to the tenants of private landlords will result in higher profit margins for the builder, seller and landlord of homes, and a waste of public funds which could have otherwise been channelled into the public sector.

The need for socialist priorities within housing, meeting the greater before the lesser need, remains imperative. In the present situation in British society, at least half the number of houses assessed as needed will be built where speculative builders find it most profitable. In a society of acutely unequal income distribution, these areas will not coincide with the areas of need. Coloured immigrants, large families, the elderly and problem families are offered only the decaying lodging houses of Sparkbrook, Islington and Notting Hill. Here the landlords are typically the 'slumlord' successors of Rachman; the children are from the 'social priority' schools of Plowden; the 'Cathys' are the families evicted from their last despairing refuge. And here too flow the prostitutes, the drug-addicts, the small-time criminals: all the elements of our society clustering in the same anonymous gloom of deprivation.

Health

The National Health Service was a major attempt, by the post-war Labour government, to establish a new standard of civilized community care. From the outset, it was subjected to severe and damaging pressures: from the vested interests of private medicine, the narrow government policies mediated by the Ministry of Health, the patterns of influence exerted by a capitalist drugs industry. Its present condition is a sufficient commentary on what has since happened, in the recovery of capitalism, to that kind of socialist objective. Dilapidated hospitals; bad pay and conditions for staff; authoritarian institutions and attitudes; a class-biased selection of medical workers; a drastic shortage of specialist workers in the overlapping fields of medicine, psychiatric care and social work; the draining of the public sector for private medical provision: all these are evidence of the disintegration. What is now happening is a fight to keep even this service going, against powerful pressures to revert to a more primitive correlation of care and money.

It is only by asserting and developing the original principle that these pressures can be resisted. The present health service reveals a conflict between two opposed attitudes: the private-enterprise conception of the individual doctor practising in his own home (to which the whole theory of private medical care is linked), and an emerging conception of community care and co-operative partnership centring on an inter-relation of medical and social needs, in which social and welfare services, public and preventive medicine, psychiatric and geriatric care could be co-ordinated into a common effort. To return the health service to its true status, at the centre of any humane society, is to demand the resources which would make possible not only the reconstruction of the most threadbare parts of the service, but also the radical remaking of existing structures in a new emphasis on community care.

Education

In education, poverty and inequality can be seen in two main ways: in the severely inadequate resources available for this fundamental social need; and in the gearing of the educational system to a narrow and restrictive conception of human intelligence which confirms and perpetuates the class structure of British society. The separation of an elitist education for the 'leaders' from a rigidly vocational training for the 'lower ranks'; the offering of false alternatives between education as liberal self-development for those not immediately vulnerable to the pressures of the economic system, and as the transmission of values and skills for a subordinate place within that system: these remain characteristic.

In 1963, 75 per cent of primary school children and 53 per cent of secondary school children were in classes whose average size exceeded thirty. In that year, only 45 per cent of children aged 15 were at school, the enrolment ratio for 17-year-olds was 13 per cent (as against 74 per cent in the U.S.A.), and in full-time higher education the ratio was only 8 per cent (as against 30 per cent in the U.S.A.). Over half our primary schools were built before 1900; the Newsom Report noted that 40 per cent of all secondary modern schools were seriously inadequate, and that figure rose to 79 per cent in slum districts. In other branches of education, there is a continuing shortage of places. Qualified candidates are still turned away from training colleges and universities.

Inequalities between different levels of the state system, and between geographical regions, are also serious. The average grammar school child has 70 per cent more money expended on him than the child from the average secondary modern school. Some local authorities are spending £100 per child, while eight are spending less than £72. A comparison of local educational authorities reveals wide disparity in the conditions of slum schools, the pupil-teacher ratio, the provision of equipment. To compare the state system as a whole with the privileged private sector is to see even grosser inequality. What advances have been made, to unlock a damaging and impoverished educational structure, have been marginal and ineffective: only 8.7 per cent of our children are at present in comprehensive schools, and it is not expected, on any realistic estimate, that all the comprehensive schemes so far proposed can be fulfilled until at least 1980. The necessary extension of the school-leaving age is at once under-financed and postponed.

The socialist alternative, of education as a preparation for personal life, for democratic practice and for participation in a common and equal culture, involves several practical and urgent measures. We need to abolish a private educational provision which perpetuates social division. We need to create a genuinely comprehensive system of nursery, primary and secondary education which will be more than a matter of 'efficiency' or 'streamlining' but will break through the existing, self-generating system of a class-structured inequality of expectancy and achievement. We need to shift emphasis, within what is actually taught, from the transmission of isolated academic disciplines, with marginal creative activities, to the centrality of creative self-expression and an organic inter-relation between subjects, between theory and practice. The existing curriculum, particularly at the secondary stage, is an expression in intellectual terms of our underlying structure of classes: specialized and unconnected disciplines for what are called academic - in fact professional - people; the fallout from these disciplines, in partial and grudging ways, for the remaining three out of four. There can be no comprehensive education until there is a genuinely basic common curriculum, which relates all learning to the centres of human need, rather than to prospective social and economic grades. The present comprehensive programme has to be defended against openly reactionary attempts to maintain a discredited selective system. But equally it will in its turn be absorbed, into a persistent class structure, if in substance and manner the actual education remains divisive. An immediate lead could be given, in the necessary expansion of higher education, by the creation of genuinely comprehensive universities. Instead of the present class structure of institutions, it would be possible to link colleges of technology, art, education, domestic science and adult education with each other and with the existing university departments: making them regional centres of learning of an open kind.

8. The realities of work

Education is now, increasingly, the deciding factor in kind and status of work. We move from one unequal world to another. Thus fringe benefits, which have mushroomed in the period of 'affluence', give the 'golden' handshake to top managers and the 'copper' handshake to the man on the shop floor. Shift working has increased, so manual workers find themselves increasingly cut off from normal social life and enduring the increased health hazards imposed. Accident rates among manual workers are increasing. Certain skilled manual workers may achieve white-collar living standards, but differences of work experience and social value keep the class divisions more or less intact. The man on the shop floor is still likely to remain there for all his working life; the middle-class man has a career before him, prospects of promotion, and a rising income. At the lower end of the white-collar scale, promotion opportunities appear more restricted than in the past, and economic levels are relatively depressed. The gap between skilled and unskilled manual workers widened during , this period of 'affluence', but with the routinization of office and administrative work, linked to the advance in skilled manual workers' income levels, a parallel gap seems to have opened between controllers and supervisors on the one hand and routine black-coated operatives on the other.

Meanwhile, in certain advanced industries, other changes in working relations are coming clearly into view. New complex technologies and large-scale integrated patterns of production require higher levels of skill, which penetrate gradually downwards into the hierarchy of the work force. As industry becomes more intensively capitalist, so the reliability and loyal commitment of labour grows in significance. Advanced capitalism cannot afford to have its vast schemes of investment, its intricately planned and co-ordinated programme of production, thrown unpredictably out of gear

by an insubordinate and unassimilated work force. The direct costs of
labour matter less, in industries which are highly capitalized; these, in any
case, can be passed on in terms of managed prices. What matters, crucially,
is that the work force should be reliable, sufficiently skilled, and at least
compliant with the process of production. Advanced corporate
organizations cannot afford relations of overt coercion, and the hostility
and rebellion which these engender.

Thus we find the development, in industries which use developed
technologies, of corporatism. Relatively high wages, guaranteed
employment, occasionally a graded career structure, higher future
expectations, fringe benefits, 'labour relations', the co-option of unions as
agents of labour discipline: these are the strategies used to create the
compliance which is technically and organizationally required. In return
for these graded benefits, men are induced to 'belong' to the firm.

These are the emergent patterns of an advanced capitalist organization.
While they come to include a larger proportion of workers - white-collar,
technical and skilled - they create also, at the bottom of the system, a much
poorer proletariat, composed both of those who are left behind by
industrial change and of those performing the most menial social functions.
These poorest workers tend not to be in unions; they are the long-term
unemployed of declining regions and industries; they are a new population
of immigrants imported to do jobs which indigenous workers will not do in
sufficient numbers.

At the same time, the industrial changes which are now urged on
working people in the name of modernization, in mines, railways and
docks, are threatening traditional communities, discarding men after many
years of work, devaluing old skills and destroying the whole life-experience
of people as capitalism has done throughout its history. Those who resist
and defend themselves, in the name of a continuing way of life and a whole
social experience, are dismissed as irresponsible, the prey of 'agitators'. Men
who are in the way of impersonal market forces - and they will include,
over the years, a large proportion of working people - are simply disposable,
to be shifted and disciplined as capital dictates. But it is not only in
conditions of technological obsolescence that men are being dismissed. The

economy has also institutionalized a periodic redundancy for what it calls the national good. In the winter of 1967-68, more than half a million people, and many more who have withdrawn from the labour market in the absence of work, were made unemployed by a cold-blooded exercise in capitalist economic planning: what is called, in that miserable jargon, deflation. It is the economy that is being deflated, but it is men and women - the exposed men and women who have to find work to live - who take the actual suffering, and tighten real belts.

It is not only conditions of work, in a general sense. One of the most bitter areas of poverty and inequality, in modern society, is our experience of what work means, as a giving and taking of human energy. It is characteristic that in modern capitalism, and in a diluted Labourism, the problem of meaning in work is hardly even discussed. What we get instead is the debased talk of human relations in industry: that is to say, the human relations that are possible after the crude economic relations have been laid down. What is now called man-management is an exact expression of this degraded technocracy; it means, quite openly, keeping people happy while they are working for you. Any other working relationship is now not even conceived.

At the centre of capitalism is the power of a minority, through ownership and control, to direct the energies of all other members of the society. It was to end this intolerable situation that socialists proposed public ownership, as in the Labour party's famous Clause Four. But as the struggle to retain Clause Four grew more desperate, the gradual erosion of its socialist content went largely unnoticed. The terms of the argument have been increasingly dictated by the opposition: nationalization has been offered as the answer to inefficiency, or as the remedy for industries hit by current crises of capitalism.

Clearly, a more rational use of limited resources is part of any socialist programme. But public ownership has always meant, too, the substitution of communal co-operation for the divisive forces of competition. It is concern for the actual social relations generated by capitalism, of inequality, mutual exploitation, mutual aggression, which has produced the socialist critique of contemporary socio-economic organization. It is this which

should be our central concern in redefining the concept of public
ownership.

For in a technically advancing economy, and in the extreme
complication and impersonality of large-scale institutions, we are forced to
choose between fitting men to systems and fitting systems to men. Against
an advanced capitalism, only an advanced socialism offers any chance of
the recovery of human controls. Men can gain more control, not less, when
the kinds of work that have been, through generations, back breaking,
frustrating, or boring can quite practically be mechanized and automated.
But if, as now, these technical developments are used mainly to reduce the
cost of labour to the capitalist, there is no good future in them; only
unemployment and loss of meaning in activity. If instead, they are used to
reduce labour itself, under the democratic controls which will ensure that
men are not simply discarded and that the released energy will be used in
active ways - a more active care for people in need; the endless work of
exploring ourselves and our world - they are the means of a liberation
which the labour movement has always imagined and which is becoming
possible. Modem capitalism, and a Labour government accepting its view
of the world, are in nothing more poverty-stricken, more attached to the
meanness and scarcity of a dying world, than in their attempts to rationalize
the priorities of machines, and to reject all perspectives which offer the
release of free human energy. In a jaded period, they can often
communicate their cynicism, or transform into enemies the very men who
in their places of work try to preserve a human priority and to assert a
human will. We believe that in work, centrally, the quality of our society is
decided and will go on being decided.

Poverty and inequality are material conditions, but they are also states
of mind, states of being. In a class society, the majority of men are seen only
as a work force, a labour market, and welfare is marginal to that, with some
minimum provision for those who have dropped out, through age, sickness,
disability, family care, or bereavement. We say, on the contrary, that we
have first to see the human needs, and then the work necessary to provide
for them. To tire a man out, to force disciplines on him, to separate the
work from the meaning, which is always decided by priorities from

elsewhere, is intolerable, yet it is what we are tolerating. Men are now poorer than they need be, in skills as much as in income, in hope as much as in security, in the desire to create as much as in the power to know. A transforming energy will only flow in our society - confident, co-operative, giving and taking in a necessary process of change - when we have got rid of a system which is fundamentally divisive, exploiting and frustrating in its basic structures, which has been so for a long period, and which in this central respect shows no signs of real change.

9. Communications

In any complicated society, social realities not only exist; they are formed and interpreted. For any actual people, including the most exposed, direct experience of the society is fragmentary and discontinuous. To get a sense of what is happening, at any given time, we depend on a system of extended communications. The technical means for this now exist in many new and effective forms. But it is then necessary to realize that the overwhelming majority of these means are firmly in capitalist hands.

It is true that most of our communications - for example newspapers and magazines - have always been in capitalist ownership. But in the present century, and with increasing effect in recent years, the relative variety of ownership and opinion which marked the earlier phase has been sharply restricted. Seven out of eight copies of all national morning papers are now controlled by three publishing combines, while seven out of eight copies of all national Sunday papers are controlled by two of these same groups and one other. Behind this concentration of the ownership of newspapers there has been a related development of combine ownership in the provincial press, in magazines and now increasingly in books. Similar combine ownership has developed to an extreme scale in cinemas and to an important extent in theatres. The important exception to ownership by a capitalist combine has been broadcasting and television. But the introduction of commercial television, which is to an important extent in the hands of the press and entertainment combines, has radically modified this. There are increasing pressures to convert what remains of public communications into the familiar commercial pattern. Within this situation the B.B.C., which traditionally regarded itself as the voice of the old Establishment, is under constant pressure, which it by no means always resists, to function as part of the new Establishment: to be the organ of a new capitalist state and its official culture.

The economic pressures in every area of communications are severe and increasing. During the 1960s six national papers have been shut down, although five of them had circulations of well over a million. With rising costs, and with the ownership of the vital raw material - newsprint - in combine hands, we are likely to see still further reductions in the range of the national press - perhaps to as few as two or three morning papers - while the survival of the Left press, already weakened by the loss of the *Sunday Citizen*, is bound to be problematical. It is a paradox of the modern means of communication, which are so essential if a complicated society is to know and speak to itself, that they are so expensive that their control passes inevitably, unless there is public intervention, into minority hands, which then use them to impose their own views of the world.

It is significant that the full elaboration of this system has coincided with the development of an electoral democracy. Of course, within a particular consensus, rival opinions, rival styles and rival facts are offered. Competition between established viewpoints gets full play. But it is then not only that minorities and emergent opinions find great difficulty in being heard on anything like equal terms. It is, even more crucially, that the continuous description of social reality is in what are clearly minority hands, with no possibility for effective majorities to articulate their own experience in their own terms. What life now is like, which can be only partly and unevenly verified from first-hand experience, is continually presented to us in a politically structured form, which it is very difficult to confront with any similarly total view.

10. Advertising

What matters, if we are to break this situation, is not only the passing of ownership into minority hands; it is also that the motive power of this concentration is advertising revenue. Indeed in many cases now, the first function of a newspaper or magazine or commercial television company is to gain advertising revenue, while the apparent content of the communication is secondary; is indeed selected and judged by its success in collecting an audience or a readership for the advertising. Whole areas of what ought to be a public communications system are then in practice subordinated to the general needs of advertisers. This advertising revenue, which usually makes the difference between survival and extinction, is often interpreted as if it were a simple support cost. But of course the money comes from the owners of capitalist industry, and it is not only this source, but the actual content of advertising, which allows us to see what looks like a straight commercial process as a system of political and cultural formation.

It is here, centrally, in the styles of advertising, that the view of life on which contemporary capitalism depends is persistently communicated. We may believe or disbelieve, be amused or annoyed by, this or that particular advertisement. But what is present throughout is an offering of meaning and value in terms of the individual consumer. Success, health and attractiveness are presented consistently as the possession - often the competitive possession - of things. It is not that this is an undesirable materialism; it is in important ways not materialist enough. The need for commodities (and indeed for accurate information about them, which advertising does not provide) is an obvious and welcome part of the development of a modern society. What advertising does is to bind the commodity to other and irrelevant values, and so to attach human need to particular and convenient versions of individual behaviour and responsibility. Thus the television documentary on poverty or famine is interrupted, in what are always unnatural breaks, to show a succession of crude images of unrelated consumption, or even of happy waste. The links between what we might all want and often urgently need, and the real ways in which, in our relations with each other, these goods are actually distributed are then steadily suppressed. We get an idea of a society in which we need ask no other questions than the name of the brand, and in which the relative importance of this man's marginal product to another man's desperate need is never questioned, while the game and the music last.

The other central view that these advertisements communicate is that we are all effectively free to choose, and that effective choice is about styles of consumption. It was in advertising, first, as a means of what the agents call 'penetrating the consumer's mind', that the idea of a 'permissive' society was propagated. With all actual constraints and scarcities suppressed, it was possible to project an idea of freedom and of the full life, which not only insulted the people suffering real pressures and exposures in the society, but also specialized vitality and fulfilment to a kind of isolated and morally justified perpetual intake. It is now clear that these images and methods, coldly worked out to persuade us to behave in ways convenient to an economic system giving priority to the production of consumer goods, have been successfully extended to what looks like normal communication. A comparison of advertising and editorial pages, in the Sunday papers, will show how far this has gone. And the circle is then almost closed, for the view of life which was hired by a set of economic interests begin to offer itself in its own right, and to seek to direct what we know of ourselves and of others.

For this is a society in which many kinds of economic and official discipline are severe, but in which the cry of 'freedom' and of 'permission' most often goes up about quite other situations and experiences. It is a society in which there is still official censorship of certain important arts, but in which the routine propagation of stories of crime and of corrupt sex is habitual, in the direct and profitable service of catching and misleading attention. It is a society in which this form of pseudo-art is repeatedly hired, but in which artists working on their own account and with different human conceptions are insulted by the question: 'can we afford to pay for you?' In real terms art pays for itself, and more than pays; it is a central part of the real wealth of the world, and is indeed treated as such in commercial speculation. The only problem in the economics of art is in effect one of arranging that the real wealth represented by established works should be used to encourage and maintain their successors. But as things now are, this wealth is appropriated, and, apart from a little patronizing support, artists are told to enter a market structured in the service of commercial interests. In these different ways, we can see in the communications system the effective priority of the institutions and interests of a new capitalism. Specific advertising has a long history, but modem 'mass' advertising developed in direct relation to the internal evolution of a capitalist system of production and distribution. Historically it takes its effective origin from a period at the turn of the century in which control of the market became increasingly necessary as the only way in which capitalism could overcome its inherent irrationality. It belongs with such systems as cartels, quotas, tariff and preference areas, price fixing and general trade campaigns. It has assumed a rapidly increasing importance in all subsequent stages of capitalist reorganization. It is always an irrational cost, in the sense that it replaces the rational dissemination of impartial information about goods and services which would be possible in a different economic system. But it is of course an inherent cost of capitalism, which has at any price to resist any general social controls over its production decisions. The maximization of profit demands that these should be made by criteria internal to capitalism, and yet an effective system of regular and predictable consumption has at the same time to be established.

Advertising is now a main means to this. It is a way of organizing and directing a consuming public, which is given real but only limited and marginal choices. As such, this institution, which has spread to gain effective control of our whole system of social communications, is a critical symptom of the formation of a new capitalism.

11. The meaning of modernization

What is this new capitalism? Its realities have been hidden from us by the central political development of the sixties: the internal transformation of the Labour party. Many of the crucial shifts in ideas took place in the fifties, but it was in the sixties, decisively, that what had been seen as Labour's historic mission, to end poverty and unemployment by transforming the existing society, was redefined, in carefully selected ways, as a call to build a rather different 'New Britain'. Our central case is that this was really the adaptation of the Labour party to the needs of contemporary British capitalism.

Many of the crucial shifts of emphasis and meaning took place around the word 'modernization'. But what did modernization mean? In the first place, it meant overcoming inefficiency - the cause to which all the weaknesses of the British economy were attributed. The British economy is indeed inefficient in many ways. But to abstract its deficiencies from the general character of British society was wilfully misleading. The problems of inefficiency cannot be detached, for instance, from problems of foreign policy, since some of the economy's heaviest burdens follow from the particular international policy which successive British governments continued to pursue. It cannot be separated from the gross inequalities, in terms of opportunity and reward, the immense discrepancies in terms of power, authority and control, between those who manage men and those who sell their labour. Neither can it be abstracted from the whole drive to consolidate a new capitalist economy which successive governments also pursued - a policy involving the emergence of larger private economic units, the control and absorption of the trade unions, the redefinition of the role of the State in economic activity. If we want to test the validity of modernization as an economic panacea, we have to see it in its real context:

as not a programme but a stratagem; part of the language and tactics of a
new capitalist consolidation.

Modernization is, indeed, the 'theology' of a new capitalism. It opens
up a perspective of change, but at the same time it mystifies the process,
and sets limits to it. Attitudes, habits, techniques, practices must change:
the system of economic and social power, however, remains unchanged.
Modernization fatally short-circuits the formation of social goals. Any
discussion of long-term purposes is made to seem utopian, in the
down-to-earth, pragmatic climate which modernization generates. The
discussion about 'modernized Britain' is not about what sort of society,
qualitatively, is being aimed at, but simply about how modernization is to be
achieved. All programmes and perspectives are treated instrumentally. As a
model of social change, modernization crudely foreshortens the historical
development of society. Modernization is the ideology of the never-ending
present. The whole past belongs to 'traditional' society, and modernization
is a technical means for breaking with the past without creating a future.
All is now: restless, visionless, faithless: human society diminished to a
passing technique. No confrontation of power, values or interests, no
choice between competing priorities, is envisaged or encouraged. It is a
technocratic model of society, conflict-free and politically neutral,
dissolving genuine social conflicts and issues in the abstractions of 'the
scientific revolution', 'consensus', 'productivity'. Modernization presumes
that no group in the society will be called upon to bear the costs of the
scientific revolution - as if all men have an equal chance in shaping up the
consensus, or as if, by some process of natural law, we all benefit equally
from a rise in productivity. 'Modernization' is thus a way of masking what
the real costs would be of creating in Britain a truly modern society.

When we ask, then, why, under a Labour government, there is still an
accepted level of poverty and inequality, and an *accepted* level of
unemployment - the very things which the party came into existence to
abolish - the answer is in this political model we have analysed. Labour
changed its values because it reduced politics to a priority of techniques,
but this was not even, in any clear way, its own deliberate choice. It was the
result of the pressures of an economic system where techniques were in

charge, in a very special way. The technology of a new politics was in fact the technology of an advanced capitalism, at a critical stage of its growth. It is this technology and its effects that we must now directly examine.

12. New capitalist requirements

Any changing technology - the changing 'forces of production' - requires new economic structures and ultimately new property relations and new institutions for its full development. We are now in an epoch of the most far-reaching changes in technology that man has ever devised. The necessity for an increasing division of labour, for ever widening co-operation in production, and for detailed planning of the flows of input and output has had profound effects.

Thus the huge scale of operation of plants and firms, integrating backwards into the control of raw material sources, and forwards into the management of the market, has brought to an end the classical political economy. Under that system the competition of thousands of producers in the market determined prices and profits and the allocation of resources to meet expressed human wants: the result being willed by none but the 'hidden hand' of the price mechanism. Giant corporations now themselves manage prices and production, the resources of capital and materials, and the very wants of the 'consumer' in the market.

Fifty companies in Britain own nearly half of all company assets. When even one of them invests in new plant, it disposes of a sizable proportion of the nation's capital investment. The decision may be crucial for the welfare of millions of people. What we have to determine are the criteria by which these decisions are made. The modern corporation is large because of the economies of scale that can be achieved by large plants using modern technology, and because of the need, in an unplanned economy, first, to control the sources of input, and, second, the markets for output. Its semi-monopolistic position allows it to charge prices which will ensure that it can accumulate much of its own new capital. Its management is increasingly professional because the processes not only of production but of finance and management involve complex techniques. Such are indeed the demands of modern technology.

But then consider the relationship of the modern corporation to income distribution. When firms were small, and many men could rise in their lifetimes to be owners of their own small businesses, it could reasonably be argued that ownership of wealth was the reward of enterprise as well as the fruit of exploitation. The modern corporation, however, is the end result of a long process of concentration in which the individual owner has become, with some exceptions, a mere 'coupon clipper' owning a millionth part of each of several giant combines. Despite death duties, or rather because death duties have become almost a voluntary tax paid only by those who hate their children, individual ownership of major wealth persists. Corporate wealth, however, is now infinitely greater and more important. The modern corporation must still maximize profits to survive in the jungle of giant competitors. It is now the main engine in our society for the accumulation of wealth.

The method of operation of the large modem corporation is essentially the method of pre-emption. It relies on the state to maintain aggregate purchasing power, its leaders having learnt their Keynesian lessons well enough to pay their taxes to the Welfare State and to the International Bank. But within the market thus sustained, the giant corporation pre-empts the best land and minerals, the most capital, the most skilled labour and the most affluent customers. Within its own sector the most advanced technology is applied, with the most skilled planning, to large-scale production for its own creation, the 'affluent mass consumer'.

It is not that the modern corporation is not interested in poor consumers, uneducated workers, poor lands. For it needs, still, the supply of cheap labour-intensive services from sectors where modern capital-intensive technology cannot be so profitably applied. The dualism of ancient and modern industry in Japan is not a passing phase but a typical example of a development that is most evident in the United States. The ever-increasing application of mechanical means to the process of production, right up to wholly automated processes, results in new industrial investment becoming highly labour-saving. Over a long period industrial investment has tended to be in more efficient equipment that was in effect capital-saving. Automated processes are labour-saving. For them to be worker efficiently and profitably in view of their high capital costs, they must be worked continuously and at full capacity, with the least expenditure on unnecessary labour. In plants with such processes the effect on the earnings of labour is that while the average net product of those at work in the process is very high, the marginal product (that is, the net product of extra men taken on) is likely to be relatively very low. It is a central part of wage theory that the demand price of labour depends not on the average but on the marginal net product.

Where such labour-saving developments occur it is evident that wages can be held down unless the skills and education of the men required are hard to find or take long to develop on the job. Profits will boom with rising productivity, while real earnings rise more slowly, as they have consistently done in the United States. Meade has described the society which would emerge as the share of profits and property income grew in proportion to other income:

> There would be a limited number of exceedingly wealthy property owners; the proportion of the working population required to man the extremely profitable automated industries would be small; wage rates would thus be depressed; there would have to be a large expansion of the production of the labour-intensive goods and services which were in high demand by the few multi-multi-multi-millionaires; we would be back in a super-world of an immiserized proletariat and of butlers, footmen, kitchen maids, and other hangers-on.

Such a development is all the more likely because the demand of the unions for work sharing, with their unemployed brothers, tends to be weaker than the demand of the employed for higher wages. This tendency is greatly reinforced by the capitalists' arguments for efficiency. To employ more men on shorter hours rather than fewer men on longer hours greatly raises overhead costs. For each extra man taken on there are not only the costs of canteen space, cloakrooms and car parking, the extra work of wage clerks and supervision, but National Insurance contributions, payments to

Redundancy and Training Funds, superannuation payments and a whole
range of other so-called fringe benefits. It is a remarkable fact that in both
Britain and the U.S.A. there was practically no reduction in working hours
in the twenty-five years between 1940 and 1965, although during this time
output per man hour was much more than doubled in real terms. Only a
few unions have fought for a shorter working week and often this is in effect
a way of obtaining overtime rates. The hours worked stay the same, and
this suits the giant corporation thrice over: the corporation pays less for its
labour; the worker buys another car or television set instead of taking part
of his extra wage in leisure; and a pool of unemployed or underemployed
workers remains outside the corporation to pull down the price of labour.

Those who cannot understand why the Labour government has not
introduced minimum wage legislation, to which the Prime Minister most
specifically committed himself before the 1964 election, or sufficiently
raised unemployment and sickness benefits and Family Allowances need
look only at Gordon Walker's explanation to the House of Commons in July
1967: welfare payments should not be allowed to rise so high as to act as a
'disincentive ... if you so arrange things that people who are not working
get more than if they are at work'. It is the same ratchet effect of wage
differentials, above the lowest paid or above those on benefit, that led the
government to decide, when in office, that 'a guaranteed minimum would
not contribute towards faster economic growth'.

A minimum wage would be regarded as inflationary because the
government would not be likely to reduce demand among the rich to
compensate for the extra demand from the poor. But it would be resisted by
business also, on the grounds of efficiency. If workers were paid more in
any sector than their net product, or what they could have produced net in
any other sector (which may of course be nil if they are unemployed), then
labour costs will rise relative to capital costs, and employers will only tend
to increase their use of machinery still further in order to save on the use of
labour. The drive of the modern industrial corporation towards
labour-saving efficiency is of course what has given us the blessings of
reduced toil and cheaper goods. But the blessings are not unqualified either
in their distribution among persons or in their distribution among

particular products. It is to this second aspect of new capitalism that we must now turn.

13. The laws of the new market

The bundle of goods and services which constitute the National Product is not constant in composition. Rather it changes through time as technological innovation renders certain products obsolete and permits the introduction of new ones. Technological change is a convenient focus for thinking about growth of the economy, for it immediately raises the question of how innovations are applied. What determines *how* the pattern of output changes through time, and thus what direction of growth the economy will take? This is a question about the selection and application of innovations, by firms at the frontiers of technological development.

What inherited economic theory has to say about this is that the direction of growth of the economy is determined by the choices of consumers in the market place: the familiar notion of 'consumer sovereignty'. Yet it is clear that such a reply sidesteps the important issue of how wants are created in our sort of society, and within what range choice is effectively 'free'. Undoubtedly, there are primitive societies in which, to use the economists' phrase, 'wants are given'. These are such things as food, clothing, and shelter: the basic necessities of existence. But in what sense are wants given for longer, lower and more powerful motor cars (as opposed to more buses)? Or for more B.U.P.A. girls (as opposed to a more adequate health service)? The hierarchy of wealth and status which characterizes our society is also a hierarchy of consumption standards, in which the realized consumption pattern of social groups at each level sets the aspirations of groups immediately below. The process of diffusion of new wants is conditioned and reinforced by advertising in which ideas of prestige and status are directly exploited. When breakfast cereals packets ask, in colour, whether we 'want to be the first family in our road to have colour T.V.', a new 'want' is being created in thousands of homes. The logic of the growth of mass consumption, in the private market economy, is that of a self reinforcing process of production for private wants: where private firms, for their own convenience, are in a position to determine the use which shall be made of available technology, and to influence the consumption habits of individuals whose purchases will determine the profitability of new products.

It is only in this context that we can understand the limitations imposed on planning when, as is the case with most western countries that have tried to increase the scope of government in controlling the economic environment, planning has been of an 'indicative' kind. What is meant by 'indicative' is that the government has only very limited command over the use of resources available to the private sector. It can draw up plans in co-operation with industry and labour, and use its powers to coax and bribe various groups in the economy to 'comply'. It cannot really force any major interest groups to do things they do not want to do.

In the case of our own National Plan, now on the shelf, the planners began by examining what the private economy was likely to do if left to itself. They did this by making two separate extrapolations of output over the period 1965-70. One was based on industries' estimates of future demand for various kinds of products (the producer guesswork method), and the other was based on expenditure projections worked out at Cambridge (the consumer guesswork method). These projections were then reconciled and used to forecast a likely pattern of output of the private sector in the 1970s, which, taken together with projections of public sector output, was then analysed for consistency in an overall macro-economic sense. Where inconsistencies were revealed, the object was to identify those activities which could be increased or decreased, in order to achieve a consistent allocation within the limits of available real resources and subject to certain key constraints (such as, for instance, balance-of-payments equilibrium).

What is important here is that expenditure on the provision of public welfare was treated largely as residual: 'what we can afford, assuming that we grow at such and such a rate'. The underlying pattern of growth of the economy, revealed in the forecasts for private expenditure and the likely pattern of investment of the private sector, was not fundamentally questioned.

To have done so would have raised awkward questions not merely about 'giving consumers what they want', but also about the sort of powers government would have to assume in order to effect successfully a radical redirection of resources in this sort of economy. In fact, the rate of growth planned for the public sector was lower for the six-year period of the National Plan than it had been in the previous six years of Tory government. The result was that the share of the public sector was actually to be reduced.

The government's failure to produce a reasonable set of social priorities is then not merely a matter of the special difficulties which have beset the economy. It is bound up in the methodology of indicative planning itself. The 'rules of the game' which prevail in Britain's economy make it very difficult to effect a major redistribution of resources from the private to the public sector without incurring the risk of substantial disruption. The decision to intervene in controlling the direction of investment, and thus the future pattern of output, would require a set of policy instruments considerably more selective and direct than the fiscal and monetary measures now available. And the application of these would have cumulative disincentive effects on the investment decisions of private entrepreneurs. The government was all too aware of these dangers, as evidenced in repeated pleas for 'realism' in planning, and for the necessity of creating a climate of goodwill and co-operation in the business community.

Thus, the debate about economic policy remains focused on very aggregative aspects of economic performance, as we may see from the N.E.D.C. Reports. Is Britain investing enough? What is a reasonable target rate of growth? How can productivity be raised? Can sufficient resources be redirected to the export sector? But the decisive questions, about the composition of investment and output, about the sort of growth we want, are made subordinate. It is in the nature of the exercise that the range of choice open to government about these latter questions is bounded by the rules which govern the successful performance of capitalism. 'Market priorities' must prevail in the course of economic growth if that system is to work at all.

Public needs then come to be regarded as residual provisions, or as a once-and-for-all cure. 'Once we have provided decent housing for all, modernized the health service, etc.' What is clear in the growth pattern of western industrialized economies, though, is that the mass consumption path set by market-led growth generates needs for increasingly higher standards of public provision, and creates all sorts of new problems as well. The locational pattern of industry has affected the pattern of urban growth, which in turn has generated major problems of planning transport flows and providing adequately located housing. The growth of private car use has not only created traffic congestion and contributed to the general deterioration of the look and the comfort of our towns, but has imposed additional costs on the provision of adequate public transport, and narrowed options of urban renewal to those governed by the provision of urban motorways and elaborate designs for the segregation of cars and pedestrians.

The failure of the capitalist market to cater for certain major public needs, while stimulating a restricted range of consumer desires, must be understood in a dynamic sense in which market-led growth creates new and increasingly serious public problems. We have not yet adequate planning arrangements for dealing with these, nor does the evidence suggest that either the methodology of current planning or the instruments at governments' disposal for implementing such plans are in any way adequate.

14. The laws of the United States economy

These are the laws and costs of the new capitalism, with the giant corporation at its centre. But what we have been discussing as a general system is also, of course, a complicated political reality. And here the central fact of this new kind of economy, to which all our institutions are being steadily adapted, is that its originator, its home base, is the United States. We shall come back to the British system, and to its unique problems: not least those of its incorporation in the extension of United States power. But what we have first to understand is the particular character of United States influence.

The assumption of world leadership by the United States was essentially the extension to Europe, Asia, Africa and Australasia of a dominance already manifest in the whole of the American continent itself. The immediate occasion for this extension was the Second World War and its aftermath. The war brought the Americans into Europe and the Far East. With an economy stimulated rather than decimated, and an ever-increasing military force, the U.S. emerged from the war as the dominant allied power, and this dominance was reflected in the Yalta agreements, as well as in the constitutions of the new international institutions - notably the United Nations, and the economic bodies of the World Bank and the International Monetary Fund.

This process was extended in the period of the Cold War, and the policy of militant anti-communism pursued by successive U.S. administrations. The formation of military alliances throughout the non-communist world, the restructuring of European and Asian economies on anti-communist lines; both these, involving as they did the manifold scattering of U.S. military bases and centres of economic guidance, further strengthened the U.S. In terms of economic strength and military technology, no western country even approached this power to prevail.

We have seen some of the internal effects of the modern giant corporation. But perhaps its most important effect, in the system of which it is the centre, is its pressure to internationalize a new network of capitalism. One of the main causes of U.S. political and ideological expansion, and of the foundations of U.S. economic strength, is the rapid expansion of private U.S. capital overseas. Total U.S. direct investment abroad rose from $12,000 million in 1950 to $44,000 million in 1964. Total U.S. holdings of foreign assets, public and private, short- and long-term, direct and indirect, are well over double this, currently standing at over $100,000 million.

The U.S. is not alone in her holding of overseas assets. Total overseas capital claims throughout the world now total some $165,000 million ($130,000 million of which are private). But, first: U.S. holdings have been growing most rapidly (in the period 1951-61 U.S. capital accounted for 71 per cent of private foreign investment, and the U.K. 10 per cent). Second, the new investment has been primarily direct rather than portfolio investment (only about 5 per cent of total foreign capital is now in private portfolios). And, third, virtually all the new private investment is made by the top 200-300 firms in the capital-exporting countries, and two thirds of it is made by the top fifty companies.

Behind these figures is the phenomenon of the international firm. Before the war there were a number of giant multi-territorial firms: Standard Oil of New Jersey, NCO, Unilevers. Since 1945 such firms are no longer exceptions. Of the top 1,000 firms in the U.S. in 1965, 700 had branches or subsidiaries in Europe. Of the top 300, there are only a handful who do not have outlets, manufacturing plants, or sources of supply all over the world. In the early post-war years this expansion was often to avoid the severe restrictions to international trade which characterized the period: protective tariffs, exchange controls, and the common preferences given to nationally based goods in the process of planned reconstruction.

Far more central throughout the period, however, was the pressure for outward expansion as the result of the *status quo* which had developed in the large oligopolistic industries in the United States by the end of the second war. In those sectors where domestic demand had become relatively saturated, expansion overseas was seen to be far more profitable and simple than sophisticated attempts to increase an existing share in the American market. It was demand, indeed, which had become the predominant concern of many firms whose ability to remain competitive depended on their ability to produce and sell enough of the product to enjoy the economies of large-scale, low-unit-cost production. As the head of General Electric announced, his company had ceased being a production enterprise and had become a marketing company.

For such companies, exporting is not enough. Often their products require after-sales servicing. Retail outlets may be limited, and consequently open to the threat of being monopolized by a rival firm (in the oil industry, for example). Alternatively, the final form of the product may have to be varied to suit the tastes of a particular country, and in such industries as chemicals, American semi-finished products are exported to Europe, sophisticated there, and sold by the branches, together with directly imported finished goods from the U.S., on the European market.

Such close links with the market are a notable feature of those industries (certain consumer durables, for instance) where European firms are already serving their borne market. The American advantage then depends on the modifications, the lowering of price, and elaborations which result from the massive research and development expenditure directed at innovation. In certain new sectors, however, innovation in the U.S. has led to the development of entirely new products. The electronic goods industry is a prime example. In such cases, U.S. firms expand abroad long before the American market is saturated, since their main aim is to cash in on what are, in form or in fact, their patent rights.

What we have been witnessing is an enormous outward drive by these highly concentrated sectors of the most economically advanced nation in the world. It is a drive for new markets, an expansion in search of demand. But because these sectors are highly concentrated, the expansion takes on a dynamic form. Some firms have expanded because of the differences in profit. But many have invested for defensive purposes. Second-ranking

American firms (Chrysler in cars, General Electric in computers) have invested heavily in Europe in an attempt to prevent a dominant American rival (General Motors and IBM) from achieving a commanding position in the new market which could one day be used to further strengthen their already strong position in the U.S.

This drive for demand, as well as the accompanying defensive investments, are the major factors behind the rapid increase in U.S. direct investment in both Canada and Europe. In Canada the figure for such investment has risen from $3,600 million in 1950 to $13,800 million in 1964. The respective rise in Europe is from $1,700 million to $12,000 million. There has also been an increasing expansion of such firms into the underdeveloped world. In Karachi one can buy twelve international brands of aerated soft drinks, from 'Seven-up' to 'Coca Cola'. Hilton Hotels are not confined to the capitals of Europe, nor are U.S. drugs, Esso tigers, or even man-made fibres. Yet, by definition, poor countries attract far less private capital for demand-expansion than the developed countries, because they have so little demand. What they do receive is usually in the form of a concession, the offer of a quasi-monopolistic position within a protected market. Thus it is that though India has drugs, her people pay more for them than anywhere else in the world.

15. The economic drive outwards

The drive for new markets is the central factor behind the expansion of U.S. firms abroad, and explains the switch in private capital flows from the poor to the developed countries. Nevertheless, though direct investment in the poor world is becoming a smaller proportion of total investment, it is still of dominating importance for many of the receiving countries, and in many cases continues to grow.

A small part of this growth is explained by what we have called demand-expansion. But the main cause has again been the nature of the oligopolistic structure of U.S. industry: the necessity for firms in certain sectors to secure their own sources of supply of raw materials.

The provision of raw materials and primary products has been the principal objective of private portfolio investment throughout the colonial period. Since the war three important changes have taken place. First, the U.S., which in many raw materials, notably oil and metals, used to supply its own needs, has been finding native resources falling short. Second, there has been an interacting process of technological change in all the advanced economies, most particularly in metals. New processes demand new raw materials, and the discovery of new raw materials or new by-products encourages the development of new processes. Some of these new raw materials are needed for critical points in the production process, yet may be in naturally short supply. Some are found in only one or two places in the world. As technology becomes more sophisticated, new rare elements enter into production, and a whole process becomes critically dependent on naturally restricted inputs. At times the threat to such supplies can have decisive political consequences, as in the current U.S. government pressure to end the Rhodesian crisis because of its dependence on supplies of Rhodesian chrome.

But in a wider sense, competition in the U.S. has led to expansion abroad not simply to obtain supplies cheaply, but because rival firms can use a monopolistic control over the supply of raw materials as a decisive bargaining counter throughout the industry. Thus, in industries such as those manufacturing aluminium or copper, even medium-sized firms have been expanding to ensure their own supply sources, while the dominant firms in the industry often continue their pursuit of concessions for pre-emptive purposes. The concessions may remain unused, but the very control over them prevents their use by rival companies.

Yet of the foreign direct investment which we are calling 'supply investment', by no means all has gone towards the securing of raw material sources. There has been a considerable movement to site plants, and stages in the production process, in locations with decisive cost advantages. It may be the availability of cheap energy supplies. It may be the presence of cheaper labour, or the possibility of saving on transport costs. In the engineering industry for example, particularly in the production of specialist equipment, the lower costs prevailing in Europe have been a major cause of the establishment of plants in Europe by numerous medium-sized American firms.

The expansion of direct investment is a decisively post-war phenomenon, in spite of the pre-war existence of overseas branches of such well-established firms as Singer sewing machines, or of overseas raw materials and mineral concessions in the hands of companies like Standard Oil. The growth of the multi-territorial firms on the current scale is decisively altering the nature of international relations. For their very size, both absolutely and in relation to the size of the economies in which they participate, coupled with their economic and technological advantages, gives them an often decisive power to impose their logic on whole economies. The turnover of these giant companies exceeds the national incomes of many countries in the poor world. Their full scale can be judged from the fact that the total value of sales of all goods and services in Britain in 1960 was only five times as large as the value of sales of General Motors. Thus in individual countries large international firms, whether singly or in groups, can occupy decisive positions either in the economy as a whole or in key sectors. When this power is coupled with the support of international agencies and the American government, decisive control of the framework of a country's development can pass outside the country concerned.

16. America and Europe

There have been two distinct periods in the post-war relations of Europe
and the United States. In the first the U.S. offered a massive injection of
both military and non-military aid. Between the passing of the Lend Lease
Act, in March 1941, and September 1946, the U.S. loaned over $50 billion
to the allies, or $53 billion if we include post-war deliveries. By 1948, a
further $16 billion had gone to liberated countries.

This piecemeal aid was followed by the sums transferred under the
Marshall Plan as part of the European recovery programme. By late 1951
this totalled 11\frac{1}{2}$ billion, 90 per cent of which had been in the form of
grants. Thus, over a decade. the U.S. had made available over $80 billion, a
massive sum intended both to sustain the allies during the war and to
rebuild their economies after it. This rebuilding, often carried through by
social-democratic governments, was intended to restore a capitalist system
in western Europe and an economic structure which would enable Europe
to take its place in what was called an Atlantic military, economic and
political community.

The main forms, indeed, which were to lead to an economic system in
which the U.S. was to become increasingly powerful in Europe were laid
down in this period as part of the package of reconstruction. G.A.T.T. was
formed in 1947 and has maintained a constant pressure in favour of the
reduction of tariff barriers between the advanced countries. Pressure has
also been maintained towards the establishment of convertibility and the
reduction of exchange controls.

The North Atlantic design was for an economic arena with as few
controls as possible, whether on capital movements or on trade. Its active
encouragement of European integration was part of this design, quite apart
from its political motives. European economic co-operation was made a

condition of Marshall Aid and led to the setting up of O.E.E.C. The European Payments Union was seen in the same light.

Furthermore, the generation and supervision of this increasingly open arena of Atlantic competition was entrusted to international agencies, the World Bank, I.M.F., and G.A.T.T., in whose original terms of reference the U.S. had a decisive say, and in whose operations they have maintained a dominant control. The point is particularly clear in the I.M.F. Keynes and the British argued that the Fund should be an automatic institution operating with a minimum of 'discretion' on the part of its management. The Americans, on the other hand, wanted politically-appointed directors, exercising control over and scrutiny of all drawings from the fund, and with discretion to promote what it considered to be appropriate domestic policies among its members.

The Americans had their way. The I.M.F. has used its 'discretion' and its power as a lending fund. Its policy has been one of marked rigidity and financial orthodoxy. When allied with the internal weight of the Bank of England and the Treasury, this has proved irresistible in the management of the British economy. Aubrey Jones publicly acknowledged that the institution of the wage freeze in Britain in 1965 was one of the strings attached to further loans by our overseas creditors. The same was true of the July measures of 1966, and of the heavy deflationary measures demanded by the I.M.F. following the devaluation in November 1967.

The first decade after the end of the war saw the economic and political bargaining power possessed by the U.S., in the relative conditions of the U.S. and European economies, and the massive transfer of funds by the U.S. to Europe, being used to construct a new international economic system. As with Britain in the nineteenth century, laissez-faire was being imposed by the strongest; by a power which could expect to gain far more than it would lose from a liberal system. Liberal economic ideology was now being turned against western Europe to her own disadvantage.

By the end of the first post-war decade the stage had been set by the American public authorities. During the second decade this stage was flooded with American private actions. Aid declined sharply. Direct investment took its place. We have already seen the extent of this new flow.

Between 1957 and 1964 the stock of direct investment increased 300 per cent to $12 billion. The flow of new direct capital which was running at $581 million in 1957 had risen to $1,752 million in 1964. In 1957 the new flow consisted of reinvested earnings in existing subsidiaries and new inflows in roughly equal proportions. By 1964 the new inflows exceeded reinvested earnings in a ratio of 3 to 1 . Furthermore all the figures are taken from U.S. estimates, and total flows, on European evidence, may have been much higher. One estimate puts total U.S. direct investment in Europe at $20 billion.

Certainly this great inflow has had a number of beneficial results. New products have been introduced, old products revolutionized and cheapened. Old sectors of European industry have been forced to reorganize themselves and improve their efficiency in the face of this competition. U.S. firms have shown themselves willing to set up in depressed areas to which indigenous firms have been slow to move. These benefits are clear and unambiguous. But the overall effect of U.S. investment in Europe threatens to be one of profound damage.

17. The technological gap

Historically, economic growth is always unbalanced. A particular sector suddenly grows very rapidly, perhaps as the result of a change in technology, or an increase in demand through improved transport, the dropping of restrictive barriers, or an overall increase in income. This growth sector has traditionally stimulated the rest of the economy. Yielding high profits, it encourages capital accumulation. It provides new possibilities for other manufactures, and new demands for inputs. In Britain, the industrial revolution saw the demand for cheap energy to run the new manufacturing industries being translated into a demand for better transport facilities. Growth is a stuttering process. New demands bring new tensions, and then new supplies.

With the breakdown of barriers to trade and the movement of capital, this unstable process takes a new form. The growth industries can be monopolized by the first country to innovate. Moreover, the tensions and demands created by the growth of this dynamic sector are solved not so much by a change in the structure of national industry, but by the leading country, which has already met these new demands within its own economy, and can now export.

This is precisely the process which Europe has been experiencing since 1945. In the inter-war period European technology conceded little to the U.S. But in the immediate post-war years, the emphasis in western Europe on reconstruction rather than innovation allowed technological leadership in chemicals, plastics, and scientific instruments to pass to the great American corporations. In the late 1950s European firms began once more to assert themselves, but not only are they still dwarfed by their transatlantic competitors; the key sectors of technological advance have moved elsewhere.

The key to the switch is the massive U.S. armaments expenditure which characterized the whole of the Cold War period. For the beginning of the Cold War coincided with two major technological breakthroughs: the discovery of the transistor effect in 1947, and the development of ENIAC, the first electronic computer. The implications for the aerospace effort were obvious. Defence contracts allowed the innovating companies to maintain their research and development effort, but by 1949 Univac were delivering the first electronic data-processing system for commercial purposes. The other firms in these new fields entered the commercial market within a few months.

At this time, European firms, while lacking the sustained contracts and the weight of financial resources possessed by the Americans, were quite capable of holding their own, particularly in the field of scientific application. But they were left completely behind as the result of two further major innovations: the development of high-performance solid-state circuits in 1956 and of the micro-integrated circuit in 1964. Each of these initiated a series of machines markedly superior to the series that had gone before. Deprived of the vital components and knowledge of the manufacturing technology, European firms were forced to continue with first-type valve machines until 1959. By the time of micro-integrated circuit innovation in 1964, the European industry acknowledged that it could no longer survive as an independent technological force.

The process we have been analysing has become known as the 'technological gap', and has been a major cause of concern to European governments and industrialists. It is linked, too, to the phenomenon of the 'brain drain'. Not only are U.S. firms able to offer better and more scientifically exciting conditions in America itself, but they also attract a great many European technologists to work in their European subsidiaries. Recently the computer firms have effected a division of labour within their international complex: fundamental research and development, together with advanced manufacturing stages, are based in the U.S. division, while the residual research work and many of the later assembly stages are distributed among its European subsidiaries. Very often European scientists, unwilling to join the American branch at first, are brought into the European subsidiary and then promoted to the U.S. branch. The temptation to leave for the U.S. is clearly much sharper when presented in this form. The brain drain, not merely overseas, but to U.S. firms in European countries, compounds the process of European technological incorporation by the U.S.

18. Effects on the 'host' nations

The international firms have their own logic. At times this accords with that of the national economy in which they operate, but often it does not. A good deal of the capital accumulated from these highly profitable sectors is ploughed back, particularly in the fast-growing or newly established industries. But considerable funds still flow out, either directly in the form of repatriated profits, or through the manipulation of the accounting prices which are attached to different stages of a process. By adjusting prices for components being transferred internationally but within the firm, an international company can take out its profits in that country where tax and transfer procedures are most favourable. U.S. oil companies operating in Britain were recently estimated to repatriate 75 per cent of their profits earned in this country.

The key point is that the foreign corporations possess the power to decide where profits are to be allocated. It may be that they reinvest them in the country which produced them, but there is always a steady flow to repay debt capital and a return on equity, and this flow can increase in times of economic disruption, and is likely to grow as opportunities for reinvestment in the sector become relatively restricted. In 1962 the outflow of direct investment from the U.S. totalled $1.5 billion; the income into the U.S. from existing direct investments totalled $3 billion. Thus the growth sectors which are central for the accumulation necessary to promote economic growth come under the control of foreign capital. It is an essentially opaque form of domination, supported in times of balance-of-payments crisis by the more transparent means of the international institutions. Nevertheless, European capitalists have been amongst the first to see American international capitalism as a generalized trend and as a threat. Some have gone into partnership with U.S. firms while they still had a strong bargaining position. Some have tried to match their U.S. competitors in the international struggle by investing in the U.S. itself. But the total figures for this reverse flow remain small. As against the $12 billion of direct investments by the U.S. in Europe, the figure for Europe in the U.S. in 1964 was $5.8 billion, a rise of only $0.7 billion from the 1961 figure of $5.1 billion.

Much of the pressure for European integration has come from European firms which not only were constricted by their national markets, but which were attempting to compete with U.S. companies. The lowering of tariff barriers has caused a flood of mergers and agreements - over 40,000 in the period 1958-64. We can expect a massive increase in an inter-country form of merger (accounting for only about 1,000 of the 40,000 agreements by 1964) once the company laws of the E.E.C. countries have been synchronized. In addition to this tendency towards concentration, not only in the E.E.C. but in EFTA countries as well (Britain's largest companies increased their spending on subsidiaries from £150 million before 1959 to some £400 million afterwards), companies will invest not according to a national interest, but where profit opportunities are brightest on the international market. The slower an economy grows, the less likely is it that profits will be reinvested in it. The heart is taken out of the growth process.

U.S. direct investment is still a small percentage of total investment in every European country, but its concentration in key growth sectors is increasingly distorting the whole growth process. For a time the inflow of new funds exceeds the outflow, but there is a pattern whereby new funds are raised from reinvested profits rather than from fresh capital inflows, and those profits not needed are transferred abroad. The new demands made by the growth sectors, instead of calling forth supplies from national industries, are met by imports. Scarce resources of highly skilled, skilled and semi-skilled labour can be drawn into the foreign-dominated sectors. A grip is sustained and tightened on the whole economy.

In Britain, where the process has gone furthest, the effects have had a decisive effect on our economic performance. Most European countries have maintained a constant outflow of long-term capital abroad. Some of the new investment is intra-European cross-investment, for the creation of the E.E.C. and to a lesser extent of EFTA have opened up market opportunities and intensified a European oligopolistic struggle. Additionally the Europeans have been attempting to consolidate themselves in old fields of influence like Africa and Asia, as well as to establish themselves in the underdeveloped parts of Europe: Spain, Turkey, Greece and the North African countries. The associated status granted to these countries by the members of the E.E.C. has had the same consolidating effect for the stronger partners as the Atlantic liberalization had for the U.S.

Europe has witnessed its incorporation into an international economic system with a hardening internal hierarchy of dominance. The overall path and the limits for European development are being set by the U.S. But within Europe, Germany is emerging as the most dominant national economy, and like its neighbours is expanding its influence in sections of the poor world. In this whole process, the public and private levers of economic power interlock and reinforce each other. The economic levers interlock with the military, and with the political. There is, too, what is evident to all, the increasing cultural and ideological penetration of Europe by the U.S. The outcome in this field is more problematical, but its influence is nonetheless felt.

It is not, we can only repeat, a conspiracy. It is the involuntary working out of a system. Given the free play of the market, low tariffs, flexible exchange control, and rigid domestic economic policies, we inevitably get the incorporation of national economies into a system whose structures are determined by the dominant economy. Thus, in the free play of the cultural market, we inevitably get the products of a sophisticated American market-oriented cultural industry.

Europe's increasing dependence on the United States is not, however, dictated by some inexorable determinism . It is governed by the options open to a European capitalist system which can be changed, and changed in ways which would break this damaging subservience. We can see already, especially in the emergence of a new form of French nationalism under de Gaulle, the points at which conflict between the cultural patterns set by U.S. economic and political penetration and the traditional cultural styles and values of Europe may develop into a new kind of cultural contradiction within European societies. A socialist response to this development is necessarily ambivalent, as it is also to the growth of nationalism in Britain. If the rejection of U.S. influence remains at the level of distaste for cultural style and value, instead of an analysis and understanding of imperialism which can be given active political embodiment, the realities of the situation are unlikely to be changed. But the potential emergence of this cultural contradiction has, even so, a value, in indicating that we are caught, not within a sealed and inevitable system of increasing U.S. dominance, but between a series of different options, which can be taken or neglected.

19. The new imperialism

Many European countries have had empires and colonies, and in the years since the war have been living in a period they call the 'end of empire'. To most people in Britain, imperialism has its immediate images: the Union Jack, the cockaded hat of the colonial governor, the lonely district officer. Few people can now be nostalgic for these images: they so clearly belong with the past. It is a recurring theme in Labour party pamphlets and speeches - how 'we gave India independence', how 'we' liquidated the Empire. Certainly, the old symbols have been dismantled: the flags hauled down, the minor royalty dancing with the new black prime minister, the new names on the atlas. The collapse of the old colonial empires is a major fact in the history of the world, and particularly in the history of Britain. But the attempted continuation of a 'world role', of a global military system, in company with other western powers, and especially the United States, is also a fact of history. What are the new and governing political, economic, military and ideological structures of this new imperialism? What is the character of Britain's deep involvement with them? What is their meaning for the new nations of the Third World?

In economic terms, it is clear that where colonial governors left off, the new international companies and financial interests took over. Similarly, the political record is more complex and ambiguous than in the usual accounts. The story of how we 'gave' the colonies their freedom comes to sound like that other story of how the rich and the privileged 'gave' the rest of us the vote, the welfare state, full employment. This story looks different from the standpoint, say, of Kenya, Cyprus, Malaya, Guyana, Rhodesia, Aden. In many cases the process by which the empire was 'wound up' entailed armed revolution, civil war, prolonged civil disobedience. In other cases, freedom came in a hurry, by political directive, almost before the national movement demanded it, while safe leaders and groups still retained power. In between these extreme cases, there were many mixed examples: suppression of one wing of the national movement, handing of power to another; imprisonment of political and trade union leaders; withdrawal under latent or mounting pressure; the creation of new and largely artificial political structures, such as federations, to bring independence in a particular way. The present complexity of the ex-colonial world is deeply related to this varied history. This is not a straight story of 'liberation' by any means.

But now a new model comes into place to explain our relations with the ex-colonial countries. This model is not imperialism as we have described it above: it describes simply a physical, technical condition - the condition of 'underdevelopment'. This is, of course, just the kind of term the system continually creates (compare 'underprivileged' and what it still calls the 'underdog'). It has a special relevance as a way of looking at a country: not a poor people, but a poor tract of land, an 'undeveloped' land. Yet others, taking up the description, can see it as the duty of a developed country to help the underdeveloped countries, as it was the duty of the rich to help the poor. Into this model of what relations between the rich and poor countries are now like, much generous feeling is directed. And when it is realized that, as is undoubtedly the case, the gap between rich and poor in the world is not closing but widening, and that with rapidly rising populations there is a profound danger of hunger and poverty disastrously increasing, still, within this model, we can only say that we must simply do more: give more aid, be more charitable. Much of the best feeling in Britain now is of just this kind.

Of course, the help must be given. But just as the Labour movement developed as a better alternative than charity for ending poverty and inequality, so, in the problems of the poor nations, we need a different perspective, and we must begin by understanding the political and economic structures of the world we are trying to change. We are not linked to the Third World by 'aid without strings', Oxfam, and Freedom From Hunger alone. We are linked also by the City of London, by sterling, by Unilevers; by gold, by oil, by rubber, by uranium, by copper; by aircraft carrier, by expeditionary forces, by Polaris.

Consider 'underdevelopment', as an idea. At its best it is meant to imply that the poor nations are rather like ourselves, at an earlier stage of our own history. So they must be helped along until they also develop, or perhaps are developed by others, into our kind of economy and society. But, in its simplest form, this is really like saying that a poor man is someone who is on his way to being a rich man, but who is still at a relatively early stage of his development. In Victorian England, some people even believed this of the poor of their time. But very few poor men believed it. They saw wealth and poverty being created, as well as inherited, by the property and working relations of their society. In the same way, we have to ask, of the poor countries: is this only an inherited, or is it also a created condition?

It is often inherited, from the familiar colonial period. Africa lost millions of its men, to the slave trade. Oil, minerals, agricultural produce have been taken in great quantities, from the poor countries to the rich. In this process, during the colonial period, the economies concerned were developed and structured for this primary purpose: that is to say, in single-crop economies or in the mining and oil-extracting areas, they became directly dependent on the world market, through the colonial powers. At a later stage, in their own internal development and from the needs of the expanding economies of the colonial powers, they became also outlets for exports and for capital investment: their development, that is to say, was as satellite economies of the colonial powers. It will then be seen that when we say 'under-development' we are not making some simple mark along a single line: such development as there was took place in accordance with the needs of the occupying powers. The poor were not just poor, in isolation; they were poor, in those precise ways, because there were rich in the world and because the rich, through political and economic control, were determining the conditions of their lives.

In fact, as the colonial independence movements were gathering force, significant changes were taking place in the advanced countries. The immediate post-war years produced a new way of thinking about the colonies. There was a switch from a predatory to a quasi-Keynesian policy. Aid programmes were initiated both by individual countries and by the new international agencies. This aid was mainly directed to the development of social and economic infrastructure and, to a more limited extent, of agriculture as well. Behind this new thinking about development were clearly political aims: concessions to the demands of the colonies themselves, linked to the belief - once the Cold War had begun in earnest - that developing economies, with more food and welfare services, would be less likely to fall to the dangers of communism. There were, too, social and idealistic motives behind the new approach, as with the rise of the welfare state.

But the new emphasis on development also linked in with the needs of the international firms. The existing supply firms had often to provide their own transport, housing, health and educational facilities, quite apart from the provision of their own police. Indeed the cost of these projects often constituted the major expense of initiating a concern. Not only did the new flow of aid lighten this burden; it helped to provide certain facilities beyond the means of a single firm - a new dam, or an international airport. Second, those firms whose principal concern was demand-expansion had an interest in development, particularly in the sectors of cheap consumer goods - flysprays, radios, plastic sandals. Third, the development plans and aid programmes were supported by, and themselves supported, a whole host of satellite firms - consultants, transport engineering, construction firms, hydroelectric equipment and so on. All these three types of international capital thus often promoted schemes for the growth of poor countries; but it was a growth without development. Almost none of the aid went to the development of an indigenous industrialization. New development was to be complementary to, and not competitive with, the economic interests of the aid donors.

American companies had had long experience of domination of Latin America through indirect rather than direct means. In the post-war years their interest was to break into the privileged markets and spheres of influence of the European colonial powers. They were handicapped by the highly preferential trading relationships of the colonial system, but also by preferential laws favouring specifically metropolitan investment in both the Franc and Sterling zones. As a result, the United States government has often allied itself with anti-colonial forces in Africa and Asia: in the Congo against Tshombé; in Guinea during the break with France; in North Africa; and at times in Indo-China (there were American officers singing on Vietminh radio in 1944, and one of Diem's first tasks in 1954-5 was to reduce French influence in Vietnam, economically, politically and culturally).

Thus European political colonialism was an obstacle to U.S. interests in the post-war period, while the European powers themselves came eventually to see that political control could jeopardize their continuing influence in particular areas. The Europeans came to understand what the United States had already learned in the American continent, that powers other than direct political control were quite sufficient to direct the broad framework of development. Detailed decisions could be decentralized to the newly independent elites, whose dependence on the old metropolis was increased by their rapid ascension to power. Thus the outline was provided, and was at last enforced by the network of power relations which we call the new imperialism.

This is the crucial feature of the concept of power which is so often forgotten by socialist and almost all other writers. It is not a simple coherent quantity, in absolute opposition to the concept of independence. The slave is not absolutely powerless; the tyrant not absolutely powerful. The degrees of their power may be understood by the amount by which each has to divert his goals when they clash with the patterns of action of others. We can accordingly construct a picture of a hierarchy of powers, each level setting the general constraints for the level or unit subordinate to it. Countries, classes, firms can thus all be dominators and dominated. Political independence may widen the area of choice in some respects and reduce it in others. And then to describe the new imperialism we have to describe the changes in this hierarchical structure.

20. The power of trade

In the colonial period, there was opposition to the setting up of any industry which could compete with metropolitan industry. Today, an essentially similar division of labour is justified on grounds of comparative advantage. The division is maintained through a fundamental principle of free trade. Former colonial empires maintain a fundamentally free-trading relationship within their territories, but restrictive trading and monetary arrangements with other countries. Sterling Area countries have a tariff system preferential to other members of the Area. Thus preferential treatment is given to imports of British manufactured goods, while Britain gives preference to imports of primary produce. The Franc Zone has a much tighter system of insulation, using a system of exchange control and import licences, as well as preferential tariffs and quotas.

The older preferential systems are gradually being eroded. Sterling Area countries have widened their preference system, and have concluded bilateral agreements with countries outside the area. The Franc Zone is being radically 'softened' through the integration of the French economy into the E.E.C., and the mutual extension of preferences by the E.E.C. and the eighteen associated African states. We see therefore an increasing liberalization of trade. Exceptions are allowed to poor countries trying to establish a new industry, though these are often used by foreign firms to give them a protected market in any one country. I.C.I., for example, established the seventeenth stage of a seventeen-stage process in the Argentine, with a *quid pro quo* that they would receive tax concessions and 100-per-cent tariff protection. When these new industries are indigenous, and produce in excess of domestic requirements, they often find protective tariffs against their products in the developed countries. The tariffs and quotas throughout western Europe against textiles from the poor countries are a well-known example. Equally notorious is the tax which Germany puts on coffee, reducing coffee earnings by an amount exceeding total German aid disbursements.

There is, then, an international trading community based on free trade, but with exceptions which, notably in the case of cheap labour-intensive manufactures, militate against the industrialization of the poor countries. Further, when so many poor countries are pressed to adopt low tariffs for manufactured goods, the chance for a successful growth industry to spread dynamic effects through the rest of the economy is severely limited. As in the relations between America and Europe, the demand for new types of input, or the supply of new outputs which might lead to a further manufacturing process, are lost to the home economy. Outputs are shipped abroad for manufacturing industry in the developed country, or the new inputs are imported. A pattern of free trade ensures that it will rarely be economic for a country to develop manufactured import substitutes. Even more rarely will it be able to compete in manufactured exports.

So the poor countries are still predominantly primary producers. And as such they have been suffering declining terms of trade: that is to say, the quantity of imports that a given quantity of their primary products can finance. There have been many reasons for this: the development of substitutes; the declining proportion of income spent on primary products; the production of some primary products within the developed countries themselves; and the lowering of prices because of increased efficiency. Meanwhile, inflation in the developed countries, the vital need of poor countries for certain imports (particularly machinery), and the linking of imports with monopolistic enterprises have all tended to raise the market advantage of the already rich. The gravity of this can be seen in the case of Ghana, whose volume of cocoa exports increased by 60 per cent over ten years, but whose export earnings remained stationary.

Moreover many countries rely on only one or two commodities: Ghana on cocoa, Haiti on coffee, Guatemala on bananas, Malaya on rubber and tin, Bolivia on tin, Iraq on petroleum. This, coupled with the fact that their trade is closely linked to one country, makes them highly vulnerable to fluctuations in price. And fluctuations have been a notable feature of the prices of these very primary products. The dependence of a country on a single commodity for its export earnings can, in the case of a slump in receipts, either force it into international borrowing or send a disruptive stimulus throughout the economy. The current inflationary crisis in Argentina, to take one example, can be traced to the effects of a sudden fluctuation in its export proceeds. Bolivia, Haiti, Pakistan, the Sudan, Iran and Indonesia have been seriously hit by fluctuations.

Through trade, then, patterns of production are set for the poor countries by the rich. This is a power manifested in the system. On occasions, trade relations can be a more direct instrument of power, notably when the trade is with one country, or concentrated on one or two crops. By threatening to cut trading relations or abrogate price-support agreements, a rich country can exercise considerable pressure.

21. The power of money

Monetary relations, similarly, have survived colonial independence, and have served as an instrument of power, as in the Franc Zone and the Sterling Area. The International Monetary Fund and the World Bank play a similar role.

The Sterling Area was formed in the 1930s, the Franc Zone immediately after the war. The Franc Zone is tighter than the Sterling Area in its rules and organization. In both areas, individual currencies are freely convertible into each other. There are co-ordinated exchange rates, and, for the most part, the free flow of capital is allowed between member states. Foreign currencies earned by member countries are normally funded in the metropolitan country. There were and still are undoubted advantages for member countries participating in these zones. At the time of protectionism and non-convertibility, both areas facilitated trade between member countries, and encouraged the flow of private capital, though the effect of both facilities was to cement the colonial bonds. They also play an important stabilizing role in the process of monetizing an economy. Nevertheless, the monetary arrangements have constituted a specific form of power in their own right. Both Britain and France have the ultimate power to block a member country's reserves. Egypt suffered this in 1946 and 1956, and Guinea's account was completely blocked when she left the Franc Zone in 1960. Again, member countries are closely linked to the exchange rates decided by the metropolitan centres. When the pound was devalued in 1949 many underdeveloped members of the Sterling Area had surpluses and if anything needed a revaluation. In the 1967 British devaluation, a number of Sterling Area countries did not follow Britain down. This reflected their diversification of trade relations, but at the same time pointed to the marked loss they suffered as a result of holding their reserves in a devalued currency. No compensation was given by Britain to those poor countries, the value of whose reserves was unilaterally cut. Britain has in fact been receiving effective loans by virtue of the reserve arrangements. Particularly at the time of non-convertibility and during the period of the dollar shortage, the surplus of non-sterling currencies earned by the Sterling Area countries served to finance the deficits of the U.K.

The free flow of capital is a central feature of the Franc and Sterling areas. The seriousness of this provision for the poor countries is not only their inability to put pressure on foreign firms and personnel to spend or save their money in the host country, and to prevent the expatriation of funds by indigenous elites. It is also that any policy which is considered by the commercial and financial community to be a sign of future instability, or of 'anti-business' politics, causes massive outflows of capital. Thus the threat of tax reform, or of the nationalization of a particular firm or sector, will prompt outflows of capital from all parts of the economy.

The control of fiscal and monetary policy is formalized in the Franc Zone, and is a logical consequence of the provision of free convertibility. The relationship of the Bank of England to other Central Banks in the underdeveloped parts of the Sterling Area is more informal and loose. Throughout both zones the pressure has been towards orthodoxy, against inflationary policies through deficit financing, restricting the issuing of credit, and so on. The Central Banks now established inside the countries (often against metropolitan opposition) have acted as agents of stability rather than of capital accumulation. This limited role of the Central Banks, particularly in the granting of credit, is compounded by the private banking network. In most countries this is made up of overseas branches of metropolitan banks, which are run essentially like any other branch bank. Credit policy is mainly decided in relation to metropolitan conditions. A rise in interest rates in London usually means a rise in interest rates in many parts of the Sterling Area. Creditworthiness is judged on metropolitan standards, and traditionally the only concerns able to fulfil these requirements have been expatriate industries and commercial trading houses. Private savings in underdeveloped countries are thus channelled to operations which accord with the colonial division of labour, and any surplus possessed by the overseas branches is transferred to the metropolis.

22. The international firm

Both trading and monetary relations have survived in the post-colonial period in a modified but still significant form. The power of the international firm has increased. We have already discussed the development of such firms, and their effect on the Atlantic economies. All that was true of the American firm in Europe is several times compounded when the investment is in underdeveloped areas.

The international firm imposes its logic on the economy of an underdeveloped country, and the effect of this imposition is almost always to put a lock on development, or, where growth is stimulated, to distort this growth away from that aimed at by the host country concerned. As in Europe, it can bid away factors in short supply, and when among these factors are the very few capable indigenous administrators, the effects on the total running of the country can be critical. The same is true of capital. Between 1957 and 1959 17.5 per cent of U.S. direct investment in Latin America was from host-country funds. Scarce savings, where they are not channelled abroad, are invested in expatriate industries. In some countries, where fertile land is a scarce resource, foreign companies annex this either for exploitation or to serve as an input to their other operations. In Zambia for example, the copper companies encouraged European settlers to farm the fertile land along the line of rail. The produce was used for those who worked in the copper belt. But the expatriate farmers became a powerful lobby on their own account, and successfully resisted attempts by African farmers to take over the marginally fertile lands and compete with Europeans in the food market.

The market dictates that scarce resources should be channelled to their most profitable use. If this use played a dynamic role in the economy such allocation would have a justification, but this is exactly what does not happen. Not only does the international firm have to import many of its inputs from abroad, but it often deliberately prevents these inputs from being developed in the country of origin. The case of technical skills is one example. Taking Zambia again, of the 498 mining technicians on the copper belt, only one was African. Of the 454 mining engineers there were no Africans at all. This is of course the result of the great poverty of educational facilities, but the firms themselves have not attempted to train key skills, since their control of the supply of key skills is one of their most important instruments in resisting nationalization.

Or take another area of major conflict between the logic of the international firm and that of the host economy. The tendency is for the international firm to export the raw material or primary produce to company plants sited in developed countries, which process and manufacture it. For the company it is economic to site its aluminium plant, rubber factory, or copper-fabricating works in a developed country, but this conflicts with an obvious growth pattern of the host country, in developing its own processing of its native materials. Jamaica provides an example. The island gained considerably from the opening up of her bauxite deposits in the 1950s by an American firm. The bauxite was shipped to the parent's processing plants in Florida. In the early 1960s the Jamaican government sought to set up its own processing plants. The extraction firm refused, and Jamaica was left with the choice of accepting the refusal or nationalizing the industry and initiating full Cuba-type sanctions from the U.S.

How can the governments of poor countries fight back? They have naturally shown themselves concerned to reduce their dependence on one particular product, though this is to demand development itself. Another instrument which has been used with great success is exchange control. By limiting an international firm's supply of foreign exchange, the firm can be induced to build up a surplus in the host country, and to invest it there, and to make every attempt to substitute for its imported inputs. But these government strategies are only possible in countries which still preserve some independent control of their planned development. In much of Latin America and Asia the process of incorporation has, it appears, gone too far for any moderate solution.

23. The effects of aid

Aid is usually thought of as the antithesis to the economic relations we have been describing. Here at last, it would seem, the generous idea of development is made actual. There is such beneficent aid, as for example in Oxfam. But the largest part of aid is held, firmly, within the overall economic relations we have been describing. And of course much that is called aid is in fact simply loans that have to be paid back, with interest.

One of the striking features of the post-war international economy has been the increase in public capital flows between the rich and poor countries. Between 1951 and 1961, of the total capital exported by the developed countries, 42 per cent was private, 46 per cent official, and 12 per cent from international agencies. We have already noted the pressures for development of a particular kind, and many of the international firms have a direct and not merely indirect interest in the flow of public capital. Currently, indeed, one fifth of all U.S. exports of goods and services are financed by U.S. government grants and military expenditure abroad. This is the result, in figures, of the common practice of tying aid for the purchase of the donor country's exports, or including a clause in the aid agreement specifying that public project work financed by the aid should be granted to donor countries' contractors. Often, when aid is tied to the purchase of goods, these are marked up to inflated prices. The proportion of tied aid is now rising, and accounts for about half of the total.

We have then to consider the effects of aid, in these and other forms. There are many ways in which aid distorts the economy of the receiving country. For example, it may be given for some capital-intensive development (involving machinery recommended by advisers from a particular exporting firm) when a labour-intensive development would often be more relevant. Again, such a project may be financed on condition

of a complementary and linked investment, from resources within the
country, when there are often more urgent priorities for that kind of
investment. Food aid, which most recommends itself to public opinion in
the richer countries, often has the effect of distorting the local agricultural
market and its patterns of production. Aid given in this and related forms
has, since it is used for consumption, marked effects on internal savings,
and on the patterns of distribution of income.

Some of these effects are inevitable, if the aid is to be given at all, but
others follow directly from the assimilation of the aid process to the
patterns of capitalist trade. Sometimes, indeed, aid has been used to control
the whole course of development of a poor country. India provides an
excellent example. The first decade of post-independence development in
India had been financed out of reserves accumulated during the Second
World War and the Korean War. By 1956, however, these reserves had been
severely diminished. India applied to the World Bank for a loan. The World
Bank stipulated the condition that the public sector should be reduced. The
Indian government refused the loan. The 1957 balance-of-payments crisis
brought India back to the World Bank, and this time she accepted both the
loan of $600 million and the conditions. She was to drop the rule that in
joint enterprises 51 per cent of control should be in Indian hands. The
most profitable areas of the economy which the government had previously
reserved for public enterprise were to be opened up to private firms:
notably aluminium, drugs, heavy electrical engineering, fertilizers and
synthetic rubber. A series of tax concessions were to be given to foreign
finns. An Indo-U.S. currency convertibility agreement was provided for.
The Indian government undertook all these, and, under the pressure of
foreign exchange shortage, the rise in internal demand and the Himalayan
war, it further reduced corporation tax in 1959 and 1961, granted
exemption for foreign technicians, and further eased restrictions on foreign
investment. As a result the whole course of Indian development was swung
completely away from its former socialist strategy.

Again, in the social development of a country, aid can have two serious
effects. It can soften social and economic tensions which would otherwise
lead to a social change, and it is of course given, for just these reasons, in

certain sensitive political areas. But in a more general way, and without such overt political intentions, aid can have the effect of perpetuating archaic social structures which badly need to be changed if a poor country is to enter the path of growth.

There is the further factor that aid is often calculated in relation to rates of return: this can mean that the project selected for aid, while clearly attractive to the lender, is not that which, independently, the country concerned would have chosen. This, in structuring a particular pattern of development, can distort independent growth, and again at times perpetuate archaic social forms.

Not all aid agreements have such effects. Some are directly commercial. Some conform to the central needs of the country: Britain granted Zambia £14 million to help her airport, road and coal plans. But to say that aid does coincide in many instances with the development plans of the countries themselves is not to deny that aid plays a key role in the control of the contours of development. It sets limits. It determines the framework. Its control, moreover, is usually cumulative. The Indian example demonstrates this. The attempts in Latin America to enforce financial and monetary orthodoxy produce results which only increase the dependence of the economies on external finance. There is, too, the necessity of repaying loans, and this usually means the incurring of new debts for the purpose of repaying the old. Such a cumulative dependence only highlights the vulnerability of an underdeveloped economy faced with balance-of-payments crises caused by short-term fluctuations of primary-product prices.

We can make, finally, a distinction between two aid situations, which can be crucial to the politics of a developing country. In a balance-of-payments crisis, or under some similar major pressure, aid has an emergency character and, as such, is often converted into a channel of power. It is in just this respect that aid belongs with the other economic mechanisms, in trade, monetary relations and the international firm, that we have already examined. Those mechanisms often produce the emergency, and emergency aid can confirm them. On the other hand, long-term aid, of a kind determined by the internal needs of a country, can, if used in the right ways, be a critical step on its road to economic independence. It is by emphasizing this long-term aid, and creating its effective conditions, that leaders of the developing countries, and socialists in the developed countries, can begin to give aid its essential meaning, and take it out of the context of capitalist trade and power.

24. Changes in the Third World

The channels of economic power interlock with and reinforce each other. They define the limits for an underdeveloped country, limits which are becoming increasingly restrictive. Balance-of-payments crises induced by export fluctuations, capital flights, debt repayments, or a rising import bill call forth emergency loans. These loans carry with them conditions promoting the further inflow of foreign capital, and also rigid and orthodox conditions on the management of the whole economy. Restrictions of money supply and deflation further restrict domestic growth, thus weakening the economy, and rendering it more vulnerable to foreign penetration, rising import bills, and private capital flight. There is then a vicious circle of new imperialist incorporation. This process is significantly most acute in Latin America. The areas of European influence are neither as advanced nor as tightly controlled. However, what we see, currently, is the extension of U.S. influence into the old European imperial spheres. The spearheads have tended to be U.S. or international aid, and U.S. private firms. This mutual reinforcement gradually softens the strict monetary and trading arrangements of the European Zones. Dollar imports and exports and dollar repayments of loans become a larger proportion of trade and payments, and increase the disadvantages of continuing membership of post-independence groupings.

It is a process not limited to any one former colonial area. The Dutch and the Belgians, in Indonesia and in the Congo respectively, have been least able to withstand the new pressures. Yet the influence of the British and French, too, is being eroded. We have already mentioned the case of India where one old British company after another is being beaten or taken over by American firms, and where the World Bank rather than the Bank of England plays the decisive supervisory role. A similar position has been reached in Tunisia, and is gradually emerging throughout the Middle East.

Pressed in Europe by the Americans, the European colonial powers have tried hard to defend their interests in the ex-colonial world. In this the French have been more successful than the British, partly because of the traditional formal rigidity of the Franc Zone, and partly because of their willingness to devote greater resources to aid. The new Associated status with the E.E.C. is a further attempt to strengthen the relative powers of the Europeans in southern Europe and Africa.

The very continuance of the power system we have called the new imperialism underlies much of the foreign policy in European countries which socialists have had to fight against so hard.

And the challenge to this formerly privileged sphere of influence feeds back to the tensions affecting the European domestic economies.

New imperialism has also created explosive tensions in the underdeveloped world itself. The rapid rise in population now threatens a worldwide famine by 1980, since food production for the native population is not a first priority in the workings of the international system. Where national income has grown much faster than population - the 'success stories of development' - the situation appears almost equally grave. In Mexico, for example, the benefits of growth have accrued to a tiny proportion of the population. Twenty per cent are now estimated to be worse off than they were twenty years ago; 70 per cent remain at the same level; and only 10 per cent have had their conditions improved. Mexico, too, reveals a trend marked through the majority of the developed world - the drift of rural population to the towns. The disguised unemployment of the countryside is being transferred to the cities and the shanty towns. Where industry has expanded, only a few jobs have been created. Sometimes the number of jobs has declined in spite of an expansion of industrial output. Those in jobs bring with them large numbers of virtually non-producing dependants. In Dakar in 1964 each worker had an average of more than nine dependants. The system is unable to deal with this massive shift from the country to the towns, with the casually employed, the dependants, and the migrating unemployed. Finally, inflation has in many countries reached proportions which are tearing societies apart.

Again those affected are less the rural population than those in the cities, involved in the money economy, with no means to maintain their incomes in the face of an annual doubling of the price level, as Brazil experienced in 1962. It is in these real pressures, formed by an international system of exploitation, that an explosive political history is generated.

25. Elites and armies

The economic system we have described has, of course, highly important effects on the social and cultural structures of the poor countries and also on their political experiences.

The development of an industrial sector in any society brings with it certain inevitable social changes: urbanization, education, the growth of new systems of social stratification. Where the industrial sector is largely imposed from outside, as was the case for most of the Third World in the colonial period, and is not part of the organic growth of the society, the blessings it brings are very mixed.

This kind of economic dualism is characterized by severe contrasts between the standards of living, expectations and horizons of the urban and rural sectors; and between functionaries in the international firms and wage earners in the primary-producing industries. Skyscrapers surrounded by shanty towns are the rule rather than the exception in urban development in a dualist economy.

The great differences existing between life within and without the elite in such a society induce a commensurately greater commitment to remaining within the elite, since the alternative is so often the near-literal wilderness. Hence the apparent sail-trimming of politicians and their readiness to switch loyalties, and the dilemma of the functionary of the international firm who becomes so dependent as to be uncertain whether he is a citizen of the firm or of the nation.

It is this penetration by the international firm, and the dependence of the elite upon it, which has robbed the national bourgeoisie of its independent political role. As a *national* bourgeoisie it could lead the fight for *political* independence, but more and more we see the formation of a *international* bourgeoisie which finds its hands firmly tied when faced with the next fight, for *economic* independence. Its very existence as a privileged group is dependent on the maintenance of the international economic structure.

In reality, as we have seen, the usual instruments of the State are not in the hands of the indigenous population. Governments are not in a position to control or plan the economy, which is subject to the extreme fluctuations of the primary commodities market. The unstable labour force thus created has its expectations raised by being brought into the wage economy, but suffers an even greater sense of deprivation when it is transformed into a pool of urban unemployed.

Even education is an ambiguous legacy of the colonial period. The grotesque spectacle of African children memorizing the names of the wives of Henry the Eighth has largely disappeared, but it does not then follow that education is now controlled by the new states. The apex of the educational systems of the Third World tends still to be the university of the old colonial power. It is largely the British university system which determines which subjects are 'academically respectable' in English-speaking African universities, and graduates can be channelled into a system of *British* educational priorities. Such a system facilitates the working of an international employment-market for the elites, which results in the Third World countries losing highly qualified personnel to international organizations, and a further 'brain drain' to the old metropolitan powers (most visible in the staffing of our own National Health Service).

The English language is on the one hand a way into a wider world and into a great cultural tradition, but on the other hand is a powerful means of binding newly independent states to their old colonial masters and of reinforcing the sharp divisions which the dual economy has created. Since the language is associated with the privileged sector of the society, the indigenous culture is seen as limited and limiting. Facility in the language of the ex-metropolitan power becomes a necessary qualification for crossing the frontier which separates the two sectors of the dual economy. The continuation of trade links established during colonial rule is greatly facilitated by the common language, as it is by an inherited system of commercial law and general business practice. The U.S. penetration of the economies of the ex-British empire is enormously facilitated by this 'bond of language'.

The essentially fragile authority which characterizes most governments in the Third World leaves them unable to cope with the contradictions created by economic dualism and the world market position, and leaves them prey to any organization in the society which has a reasonably effective hierarchy of authority, can command loyalties and, perhaps most important, has an efficient system of communications. Increasingly, armies have appeared in this role in the countries of the Third World; in some areas, like the Middle East, as a direct consequence of that particular quest for markets, by the arms industries, which we hear of as 'arms races'.

As an example of both cultural and technological ties to the metropolitan countries, armies exhibit many of the features to which reference has been made. Language and tradition, as well as bilateral agreements, make it almost inevitable that senior officers in these armies are trained at the military academies of the ex-metropolitan powers and that additional experience will be provided by observing NATO or similar exercises. Analogous to the internationalization of the bourgeoisie, we can see an increasing internationalization of the military elites through incorporation into supranational groupings such as CENTO and SEATO. The concepts of political order and stability learned there will be those defined by the ex-metropolitan powers or - much more likely - the Central Intelligence Agency. The equipping of these armies, instruction in new techniques, maintenance and the supply of spare parts are again likely to be in the hands of the ex-metropolitan power and serve to reinforce other ties. They also make it more likely that the army will stand out as the most technically advanced and ambitious sector in the society.

The temptation then to assume political power, with the normally expressed aim to wipe out just that disorder which we have characterized as the essential contradictions of economic dualism, is all too often irresistible. Disorder is blamed on subversion, subversion is equated with communism and armies are not allowed to remain neutral for very long in the struggle for 'winning men's hearts and minds'.

26. War and Cold War

Socialists have traditionally seen war, in the twentieth century, as the conflict of rival imperialisms: for colonies, for trade, for spheres of influence. But this situation was already modified by the Russian revolution, and international politics, for a generation, came to be dominated by reactions to this new factor - the existence of a socialist state - and its associated movements. The Second World War, like the First, began in Europe, but it was already different in character. The old national and imperialist rivalries co-existed with the complicated process of political struggle between socialism and, on the one hand, liberal capitalism, on the other hand, fascism. Before the war ended it was further complicated, in the Far East, by an imperialist conflict, of a new kind, following the powerful and convulsive Japanese invasion of much of Asia.

Even in the last months of the European war it became apparent that co-operation between the socialist state of Russia and the liberal capitalist states of the West would last no longer than was necessary for the defeat of the common enemy. Nevertheless, the Cold War which then commenced and which has, for twenty years, overshadowed civilization with threat was never the simple confrontation between political and economic systems which apologists of either camp wished their own peoples to suppose.

Millions of people in the West, including many in the working-class movement, were brought if not to participation at least to acquiescence in the Cold War, on the understanding that it was an essentially defensive operation. Russia was portrayed as an aggressive imperialist power, subverting western states by promoting revolutionary activities within their borders, while threatening them militarily with the might of a fully mobilized and victorious Red Army. According to this myth, western Europe maintained her independence only as a result of massive American aid, and by the adoption of a policy of 'containment' which had as its ultimate sanction the newly developed atomic bomb.

This account had never been true, even from the beginning. For the popular resistance movements in occupied Europe during the Second World War can be seen as agencies of Soviet imperialism only by the most grotesque historical distortion. They constituted authentic popular movements, with authentic revolutionary aspirations, germane to those which brought Labour's own sweeping electoral victories in 1945

Indeed, far from giving overt and covert support to these movements in the immediate post-war period, Stalin was careful to withhold support from all revolutionary movements in western or southern Europe where these might conflict with the agreements as to spheres of great-power influence entered into at Yalta. The socialist case against Soviet policies in the West during these years is not that these were guilty of adventurism but that they sought to subordinate indigenous revolutionary movements to the overall needs of the U.S.S.R. for security and reconstruction. Thus the Greek resistance movement received neither aid nor encouragement from the Soviet Union when challenging the reimposition, by British troops, of a royalist régime which was acknowledged (as by The Times of 17 April 1945) to be opposed by four fifths of the population. In France and in Italy the Communist parties pursued 'popular front' policies which involved dismantling the organization and undermining the *élan* of the resistance. In Britain, also, the Communist party, in February 1945, called for a continuation of coalition rule under Churchill in the period of post-war reconstruction: a gigantic misjudgement of the mood of the people which, it should be noted, was shared with Labour ministers in the War Cabinet. Even in Yugoslavia, Stalin assented to Tito's assumption of power with reluctance, as he was later to regard the communist victory in China. In subsequent years both Yugoslavia and China were to show how far indigenous revolutionary movements were removed from Soviet 'imperialist' control.

Thus the myth of Soviet-inspired communist subversion is a crude falsification of the complex power politics of that time. Moreover, the myth of a direct military threat from Russia was even more baseless. We have seen already that United States imperialism emerged from the war in a position of overwhelming economic strength: and this strength was backed by very strong conventional armed forces and the exclusive possession of the atomic bomb. Russia, which had borne the brunt of the struggle against Germany, was devastated by a war in which 15 to 20 millions had died. Manpower was desperately needed for domestic reconstruction, and the need for recuperation dominated Soviet diplomacy. George Kennan, the author of the policy of containment, has now admitted that 'it was perfectly clear to anyone with even a rudimentary knowledge of the Russia of that day that the Soviet leaders had no intention of attempting to advance their cause by launching military attacks with their own armed forces across frontiers'.

It was not Soviet aggressiveness but the desire of American political and military leaders to exploit to the full their position of dominance in the post-war world which signalled the first onset of the Cold War. Roosevelt's conciliatory policies had been grounded upon the need for Soviet support in defeating both Germany and Japan. By July 1945 (Potsdam) - after the death of Roosevelt - these considerations were no longer operative and, above all, America was in sole possession of the atomic bomb. It was in these circumstances that the West (Truman at Potsdam, Churchill at Fulton) made new demands upon the Soviet Union. These attempted, first, to roll back the Soviet sphere of influence in Eastern Europe (Rumania, Bulgaria and Poland); second, to modify allied policy towards Germany, where alliances between U.S. and German capital were already forming; repudiating earlier agreements upon reparations and placing emphasis less on the abolition of Nazism than on the re-creation of the economic and industrial institutions which had brought it into existence.

From this point, a complex degeneration in the relations between the two power blocs commenced. Even though the Cold War has subsequently been transformed in character and in intensity, it is necessary to recall the circumstances of its origin for several reasons. First, the myth of sole Russian - or 'communist' - responsibility for its origin continues to play so large a part in western ideology today that it must be rebutted. In this myth successive phases of the Cold War are confused and conflated. Thus

Churchill's Fulton demands (1946) upon the Soviet Union to evacuate
Eastern Europe are presented as if they were occasioned by the hardening
of Stalinist control in these countries symbolized by the *coup d'etat* of
Prague (1948); whereas, in fact, the Stalinist repression of liberal,
social-democratic, and (at length) communist opposition in Eastern Europe
was, in some part, a consequence of the siege mentality and political
degeneration occasioned by western pressure. Or, again, the Berlin
blockade is presented as the occasion for, rather than a consequence of,
United States support of Western German resurgence. Secondly, it is
necessary to recall the role of United States imperialism even at the
beginning of the Cold War, since this throws light forward - to Korea, Iran,
Guatemala, the Lebanon - just as more recent events - Cuba, Vietnam -
throw light back upon its origins. And, thirdly, socialists must see that the
Cold War, in its origins, arose from a context within which authentic
popular and revolutionary initiatives had become subsumed within a great
power conflict which cramped and distorted their expression and falsified
their direction.

It is this condition which proved to be, in the early years of the Cold
War, so deeply confusing to western socialists. For, even if the role of
United States imperialism could be clearly seen, it was never possible to
give a simple assent to Soviet communism as the protagonist of socialist
policies. The actual progress of Russian communism, under severe
pressures - internally, in the rapid fight out of backwardness; externally, in
the invasion and hostility of the old powers - had long been of a character
to check all easy, utopian assumptions. Many features of this communism
could not be recognized as anything but hostile to socialist ideas nurtured
in a more temperate historical experience. Long before the Cold War
commenced the communist parties outside Russia had passed from the role
of defender of the first socialist state to that of apologist for some of its most
indefensible authoritarian features.

As the Cold War degenerated to the brink of world nuclear conflict
(during the Korean war), so there was a corresponding degeneration in
ideology and political morality within both protagonists: in the United
States, from the Rosenberg trial to the McCarthy era; in the communist

bloc, the last years of Stalin, the Rajk, Kostov, and Slansky 'trials'. Each crisis strengthened the advocates of 'hard' policies within either camp, gave greater influence to the military lobbies, and led to an intensification of the repression of dissident ideas and groupings. Meanwhile the communist parties of the West, and their associated movements, became neutralized and discredited, politically and intellectually, not because of the priority which they gave to the fight for world peace, which was a necessary priority for any socialist; but because of their subordination of strategies to the local demands of Soviet diplomacy and, above all, because they were deeply compromised by their apologetics for the idiocies and crimes of Stalin's last years.

By the mid-1950s, the Cold War, through sheer weight of matching nuclear terror, had fought itself to a standstill in Europe, bringing with it a general deadlock of all popular political initiatives. We believe that we were right, in that situation, to identify nuclear weapons as the immediate and major danger to civilization and indeed to human existence. We were right to demand British withdrawal from a nuclear strategy, and to offer this as a positive political and moral initiative. We had to choose, and had always needed to choose, even in the worst period of Stalinism, between rival world political orders which, in the sheer weight of their military power, made any unambiguous choice virtually unbearable. That was the instinct of the simple call for unilateral nuclear disarmament: to establish a human choice where no fully supportable political choice existed.

27. The Cold War moves outwards

Under a similar unbearable pressure, the monolithic unity of the communist camp was broken through in 1956. Recognizable human voices were heard once again within the communist parties, demanding a return to political and moral principle. Democratic pressures were initiated which, although seriously reversed by the repression of the Hungarian revolution, have continued to assert themselves ever since. If the Cold War had remained as it had been in its origin, a primarily Europo-centric conflict, there might have ensued, ten years ago, some relaxation of tension; the arbitrary division of Europe might have been broken down by piecemeal initiatives from East and West; and communists and socialists within both halves of the continent might have rediscovered common strategies and objectives. This proved to be impossible. For, already, with the communist revolution in China and the Korean war, the Cold War was moving away from Europe, although leaving it in a state of impotent, unmotivated deadlock, and centring upon the formerly colonial world. In doing so, it was changing, radically, in its character and objectives.

Most people in Britain have been painfully slow to realize the altered character of international relations in the sixties, the new and enlarging sources of political disequilibrium out of which dangers of war will arise, and the new calls upon our solidarity as the Cold War has moved outwards: from old metropolitan Europe to the newly awaking continents. Indeed, the very term - the 'Cold War' - has become a falsifying, obstructive concept; for, in the new era, we must hold simultaneously in view two very different, although inter-related, phenomena: on the one hand, the massive polarized technology of the cold deadlock: on the other hand, a dozen shifting foci of hot wars,.fought with the utmost brutality and - on the side of the poor - often with the most primitive military equipment. On the one hand, there is the Polaris submarine awash in Holy Loch; on the other hand, there are the guerrilla *focos* and the terrorist intrigues of the C.I.A. In the preparation of a super-war, it is generally true that the trajectories of deterrence run between the great industrialized cities of the North and the West; but in actual war the real blood is being shed in the East and in the South.

In one sense, the cold deadlock is no more than the continuation of the policies of Yalta by other means: the division of the world into mutually agreed spheres of influence - an agreement backed by ever-more-terrible threats of sanctions against the trespasser. At this level, it has become a stabilized, even routine, affair. The heads of state can make genial diplomatic exchanges over the 'hot line' while, on each side, the civil servants exchange memoranda on overkill, and the scientists elaborate more devastating military devices. But, even if we leave larger political factors out of account, this seeming stability rests upon a delicate equilibrium - the necessity that precisely this equilibrium of deadlock should not be suddenly disturbed by one or the other side gaining major strategic or technological advantage. In 1961 Schelling and Halperin noted:

A main determinant of the likelihood of war is the nature of present military technology and present military expectations. We and the Soviets are to some extent trapped by our military technology. Weapon developments ... have themselves been responsible for some of the most alarming aspects of the present strategic situation. They have enhanced the advantage, in the event war should come, of being the one to start it, or of responding instantly and vigorously to evidence that war may have started. They have inhumanly compressed the time available to make the most terrible decisions.

Since 1961 the network of missile, anti-missile, satellite and anti-satellite weapons has become more dense, and the time for decision more hair's-breadth. Thus the Cold War contains within itself, simply in terms of its own rationale and technology, dangerous hysteric tendencies.

Meanwhile, the political basis out of which this armed stasis arose has changed beyond recognition. One part of the change was signalled by the consolidation of the Chinese revolution and the first confrontation between

Chinese and American forces in Korea. It was already apparent, then, that the Soviet Union could no longer guide, or manipulate, revolutionary movements in the old kind of way. Even old-fashioned western apologists of the Cold War have ceased to pretend that all revolutionary initiatives stem from a unified, Soviet-directed, global strategy. China, by 1957, was publicly making clear her independence of that strategy; and was adopting a revolutionary stance, more in the tone of her propaganda than in her actual actions, which embarrassed the Soviet Union in its traditional pursuit of a stable *status quo* underwritten by a great-power *détente*.

Another part of the change was signalled by the Cuban revolution - a revolution which owed little to Soviet inspiration but which was impelled, far more, by direct opposition to American imperialism in its complaisant alliance with the brutal and corrupt parasitic régime of Batista. For ten years the crucial confrontations have no longer been between the United States and the Soviet Union, except, briefly and typically, when the Soviet Union sought to take strategic advantage of Cuba as a missile base; but between U.S. imperialism and popular revolutionary movements within the poor nations.

In Asia, the United States has built up a chain of allies and satellite powers on China's peripheries - Japan, South Korea, Taiwan, the Philippines, Thailand, Laos, Saigon, Pakistan. Indonesia has been rapidly moving towards inclusion. Indian neutralism had already become unviable before Nehru's death and the Sino-Indian border dispute. In Latin America where the United States has for long enjoyed an unchallenged economic hegemony, an inter-American military command was brought into existence, underpinned by aid programmes, by direct political intervention and extensive counter-revolutionary training. The threat offered to U.S. imperialism by the Cuban revolution may be seen in the steeply rising curve of the Military Assistance Program to Latin America, rising from a mere $200,000 in 1952, to $54 million in 1959 and $121 million in the Cuban crisis year of 1962; a programme soon to be expanded again, with the supply of new kinds of weapons. In Africa, U.S. military aid and capital poured in as the older colonial powers pulled out: the first ideological military confrontation here was in the Congo.

In the interregnum immediately after the liberation of Asian and African peoples, a neutralist bloc of nations emerged, and the term 'non-alignment' seemed to be of value. In fact, the West remained the final arbiter as to what kinds of non-alignment were acceptable and what kinds were not: the use of regular and irregular 'western' military contingents by Tshombe and Mobutu in the Congo was 'acceptable'; the request by Lumumba to the Russians for help in the transport of his troops was not. In several of the military *coups* in minor African states in 1964-7, United States endorsement or aid has been dependent, not upon any profession of democratic intentions, but on the expulsion or ritual denunciation of the Chinese. Thus, in effective terms, the West established a definition of what types of political régime, what kinds of economic reform, what style of foreign relations were 'safe for democracy' in the Third World: and took the means - by direct economic and military pressure, and by indirect subversion - to make those definitions operative.

As a result, non-alignment has become progressively illusory. In some cases the United States has intervened directly. But the new imperialism does not require everywhere a direct political and military presence, as the older style of colonialism did. A measure of local autonomy can be permitted, especially where the régimes are 'sympathetic', that is 'pro-West' in character. The smaller and weaker states are held within the control of United States strategies like iron filings within a magnetic field-of-force, by the sheer ascendancy of the economic imperialism we have analysed. In this situation, where resistance is so difficult and so costly, it is all the more remarkable that several poor nations pursue, as they can, independent and radical policies, individually and collectively (we might instance Tanzania and several important initiatives in O.A.U. and UNCTAD). But then, of course, this is no longer a passive 'non-alignment', in the older sense. These nations are acting in their own interests, and those of their oppressed neighbours, in their own sphere.

28. Political managers of the world

Can this sphere be held? This is now the critical question. The economic relationships, of an international capitalist economy, have been maintained within the framework of a global system of military and strategic containment. But in the past few years, American policy has become more activist, mounting direct political pressure, the training of counter-revolutionary forces by the C.I.A., economic blackmail and, in Vietnam, major war. The choice for the Third World countries has become increasingly stark: either to be within the global orbit of imperialism or to be against it. The rapid toppling of régimes in the Third World in the past two years - in Brazil, the Congo, Indonesia, Ghana, the Dominican Republic and Guyana - signals the successes of the new hard line.

But it signals, also, the increasing insecurity of this imperialism. The Chinese and Cuban revolutions, inserted into the eastern and southern hemispheres, offer models of revolution far more attractive to the peasantry and the poor of the former colonial world than does that of Russia. Partly under the inspiration of these examples, and partly as a consequence of direct resistance to imperialist economic and political pressures, authentic popular and socialist initiatives, notably in Asia and in Latin America, have multiplied and diversified. Moreover, an ideology and culture of resistance to imperialism has arisen: a culture of the poor, the exploited, and the coloured, articulated by an intelligentsia which has moved through nationalist to revolutionary positions. The client régimes of the Third World are now seen as accessories of imperialism. A line is drawn, not between the oppressed 'nation' and external imperialism, but between the military-bureaucratic régime, captive to imperialism, on the one hand, and the people on the other. This culture of resistance now makes itself felt from Black America to Angola, from Guatemala to Vietnam. In this place and that, in recoil from the oppression and racialism of the white imperialist powers, it voices a counter-racialism; the identity of the coloured and the oppressed, as against the rich white powers.

Thus, at the moment when the West thought that Soviet communism had been 'contained' within the stasis of the Cold War, the Chinese and Cuban revolutions presented a far more direct challenge to United States economic and political hegemony. It is a challenge the more multiform and pervasive in that it is in no sense centrally inspired and controlled (and therefore subject to top-level great power accommodations). Instead, it is intricately interwoven, in ideology and culture, into the nationalist and counter-racialist aspirations of the peoples of the Third World.

Nor can this challenge be contained by the simple expedient of substituting China for Russia as the main enemy. It is true that this substitution has long been made, in United States military thinking: despite China's prolonged restraint during the Vietnamese war, she is continually presented to the West as an expansionist imperialist power. And we live now continually under the danger that the 'hawks' of the Pentagon will take advantage of the Sino-Soviet dispute to provoke nuclear war in the Far East in order to strike at China before her vast productive potential becomes realized. But even if this danger is averted, the insurgency of the 'have-nots' will grow in strength in direct response to each twist of imperialist exploitation, and in the same ratio as the gap between themselves and the 'haves' grows wider. Already we are approaching the eighth decade of the twentieth century, in which, agronomists and demographers have predicted, major famine conditions may be expected, from India to Brazil. Whether the culture of counter-racialism grows also will depend, in a direct way, upon whether the white industrialized nations are seen to be in the role of oppressors: or whether movements of sympathy and solidarity grow *within* these nations, which are not only articulate but are also *effective*, in terms of aid, fair trade, and diplomatic power.

Thus no simple unilinear analysis, of what used to be the 'Cold War', is sufficient to understand its new incandescent forms. There is an intricate interlacing of economic, military, political and ideological factors. On one hand, the lines of military strategy may follow directly upon those of economic interest: oil in the Middle East, United Fruit in Central America. On the other hand, some of the giant companies have annexed the political conflict as a base from which they can really plan, secure in the prediction of enormously profitable war contracts. The disputes within the White House and the Pentagon which led up to the dismissal of McNamara turned upon the biggest jumbo-sized contract in the history of world capitalism: a $5,000 million 'Chinese-orientated' anti-ballistic missile system. The military-industrial lobby won, and already it is being suggested that this is a 'first instalment' upon a $50,000 or even $ 100,000 million project.

At one point, strategic considerations from the older Cold War may take priority (missile bases in Turkey); at another point, the 'domino' theory made vicious by ideological panic (23,000 U.S. troops landed in the Dominican Republic within a week to deal with 4,000 purported 'communists'). In this place or in that, the involvement of American imperialism can be seen to be derivative from direct economic interests; but it would be an error to suppose that all actions will be related to this prior interest; they could, indeed, contradict this interest. For the War itself has an independent logic and inertia - what C. Wright Mills once called 'the military metaphysic' - as an ongoing system superimposed upon other, more particular, interests.

It is this inertia of an immense constellation of imperialist interests, supported by an ideology which has long ceased to calculate objective interests but which sees the postures of 'defence' as inherently those of virtue, and underpinned by a supremely complex and costly military technology which is in its own right a major war interest, that gives to the Cold War, now, in 1968, its rationale. A similar military, bureaucratic, and ideological constellation compresses the economic and political life of the Soviet Union, and imposes its hegemony upon the East European nations; but since it is not supported by the internal dynamic of private profit nor, outside the Soviet block itself, of economic imperialism, it is, ultimately, less dangerous and more defensive in character. What occasions today the greatest danger of the actual eruption of the third and final World War is not a disequilibrium between these two great-power systems, although this danger still exists. It is that the confrontation of the systems should be brought to a climax at one of the places of hot war provoked by resistance to United States imperialism.

It is, exactly, in this larger context that we must see the Vietnam war: not as an isolated case in itself, but as an outstanding and brutal example of the political strategy of the new imperialism. What is wrong in the Vietnam war is not only that it is pitiless and brutal, calling forth, as it must in every humane person, an answering cry for peace. It is also that it is a war consciously fought, by the United States, as part of an international struggle: an international test case. United States commitment and intransigence in Vietnam, in the face of an appalled world and of growing opposition at every level from the American people, are intended to signal - not to Hanoi, not to China, but to revolutionary movements from South-east Asia to Latin America - the consequences that will flow from any direct challenge to United States hegemony. The restraint shown by the Soviet Union in this conflict has been occasioned by the realization that if the immense military systems of the older Cold War should come into coincidence in Vietnam, nothing could prevent global conflict. With each sortie by American bombers deeper into North Vietnam, the United States militarists have been gambling with the lives of millions. Their bets have been laid, not upon communist 'aggression', but upon the restraint and realism of the Soviet and Chinese governments. For this reason the Vietnamese people have an even greater, more compelling, claim upon the solidarity of the people of the United States and of Europe. In receiving the full brunt of American military force without calling for the aid of corresponding Russian or Chinese forces, they are, paradoxically, depending upon the resolution of the conflict to come, ultimately, from the mobilization of world opinion - opinion brought to bear, in the end, within the heart of the aggressive West.

The mobilization of this opinion is our business. And, in this context, it cannot be sufficient to limit opposition to United States policy to its particular manifestations in Vietnam. The complicated and deeply rooted alliances and institutions of the whole Cold War period provide a dense political reality, which cannot be opposed by moderate policies but requires an absolute and exposed decision; for or against. That is why we cannot confine our critique of current foreign policy to local amendments and qualifications. We have to reject the whole world-view, and the consequent alliances, on which it continues to be based. Our problems are not, as they are so often presented, those of the last stage of Britain's withdrawal from an imperial position. They are those of a continuing stage, in what if unchecked will be a very long conflict, of Britain's participation in an international military alliance against the colonial revolution and its allies.

29. Backlash in Europe

Thus our indictment of the Cold War cannot be separated from our indictment of the new imperialism. Both co-exist; both are intricately related: it will be death if both should fully coincide. Moreover, this imperialism is not only something which is out there: thousands of miles away in Latin America or Asia. Because the main arena has passed away from Europe it does not mean that Europe is no longer centrally involved. Europe received, in 1967, a brutal reminder of the cumulative effects on a nation's political and social life of twenty years of subordination to Cold War priorities. In 1947, in the midst of a bitter civil war which British armed opposition to the resistance movement had done much to provoke, Britain handed over economic and military responsibility for Greece to the United States. This provided the occasion for the declaration of the 'Truman Doctrine' which has been used in justification for a score of interventions in succeeding years:

> One way of life is based upon the will of the majority, and is distinguished by free institutions, representative government, free elections, guarantees of individual liberty, freedom of speech and religion and freedom from political repression. The second way of life is based upon the will of a minority forcibly imposed upon the majority. It relies upon terror and oppression, a controlled press and radio, fixed elections, and the suppression of personal freedoms.

Whatever plausibility this doctrine held in 1947 dissolved into ironies as tanks encircled Athens in April 1967. For, in the previous twenty years, American 'aid' ($1,238 million in military aid between 1946 and 1958) had served to bolster a series of corrupt and anti-democratic régimes. This aid provided the real basis upon which the military elite, traditionally the stronghold of Greek reaction, could strengthen its power: a military force 180,000 strong, equipped by the 'free West', was built up within a nation of nine millions. Whether the colonels seized power in Greece at the instigation of the C.I.A. or whether United States diplomats would have preferred a more 'democratic' royalist façade to replace Papandreou's liberalizing government is not a point of substance. What is substantial evidence is, first, the political consequences of successive transfusions of 'aid' to the controllers of the military apparatus; second, the complaisance of the United States and of Britain in the aftermath of the *coup*. Despite protests from the Scandinavian nations, both military aid to Greece and NATO membership have been sustained. In Britain a Labour government has shown more distaste for British demonstrators at the Greek Embassy in London than they have for the Greek colonels who are holding thousands upon the bleak prison islands without trial.

Less than a year before the colonels' *coup*, the *U.S. News and World Report* (8 August 1966) furnished us with another irony:

> Vietnam is viewed [by President Johnson] as the 'Greece' of South-East Asia. Just as Europe was unable to relax and forge ahead after World War II until after Red aggression had been stopped in Greece, so it is felt that Vietnam holds the key to a release of forces for large-scale development and progress in Asia.

But the question, in Greece as in Vietnam, is now unambiguous: *which* forces are to be released? Britain is now playing no more than the role of a client imperialism: against the forces of colonial liberation, of democratic and revolutionary insurgency, and within the forces of militarism and imperialism. Even in the strategy of the older Cold War, Britain has been reduced to the status of a client military power. Within western Europe, the confidence of United States strategists has long since shifted from Britain to Western Germany. Lacking the nerve to make even a rhetorical gesture of independence, and to follow France out of NATO, Britain has been assigned her role: to sweat her overtaxed economy as a missile and Polaris base; to keep a large navy, and contingency bases in Europe and the Mediterranean; and to maintain troops in Germany and in the NATO European Command.

Until the early 1970s, the forces east of Suez - in Singapore, Malaysia and the Gulf - must also be maintained.

In this ongoing system of war, we are all of us, every day, involved. It is not a question of giving or withholding approval for this or that manifestation of imperialism or of social revolution. What matters, we repeat, is the choice: for or against. Only when this choice is made, unambiguously, and supported by effective action, can our criticism of particular forms have any meaning.

We have such criticisms - and profound criticisms - of communist forms and communist ideology. We shall return to these. But, equally, we have no doubt as to our choice: it is against the new imperialism. And this is an imperialism which is, already, in our own midst. It is not only that our political and intellectual life has been penetrated, in a hundred discrete areas, by Cold War agencies like the C.I.A., which evade even rudimentary democratic controls, and which recruit and operate the mercenaries of anti-communism. It is also that in the financial difficulties over sterling, and in the increasing penetration of the British economy by United States capital, pressure to support particular policies can be put on us, directly, in ways not unlike those of the new colonialism and imperialism in the most backward parts of the world. This is why, again, we see Britain's crisis as single and integrated. The fight against imperialism on an issue like Vietnam is substantially linked with the fight against direction of our own economic and political policies, not only by the Americans, but specifically by the international institutions of monopoly capital which include elements of our own society. In fighting anywhere, we are fighting everywhere.

30. The British crisis

We have now seen the world system within which a Labour government in Britain has had to work. By the 1960s, Britain had become a rather weak member in the second rank of capitalist powers, increasingly dominated by United States capital but still dominating the economies of a group of small and far less developed countries. Although most of the colonial empire had gone and Commonwealth partners increasingly turned to the U.S.A. for finance and trade, there remained a few lands to provide the resources for sustaining the role of sterling as a world currency. The problem for British capitalism, once the workshop and then the banker for the greatest empire in the world, had long been how to reconcile the roles of banker and trader. For the banker, the rate of return is the crucial question; for the trader, the growth of his trade. Since the war the City has flourished and industry has declined.

Through the whole period from 1955, high interest rates (never below $4\frac{1}{2}$ per cent) were attracting funds to the City of London, which were then invested abroad for an even higher long-term return. By 1960 the outward flow of long-term capital exceeded £400 million, with only £150 million flowing in from outside. The gap was plugged as usual by short-term borrowing. The Tories claim that there was an aggregate surplus in the balance of payments during their years of rule. In fact there was on current account a small average annual surplus, but on capital account there was a large annual deficit. Table 1 summarizes the balance of payments on average, and in the three years of heaviest deficit, between 1952 and 1964.

It can be seen that while on average, over the period of Tory rule, there was just a balance of goods and services taken together, and property income from overseas just exceeded government spending, the net outflow of long-term capital had still to be largely covered by short-term money. In

Table 1: UK balance of payments summary

	Average 1952-64 (£millions)	1955 (£millions)	1960 (£millions)	1964 (£millions)
Balance on goods	-177	-313	-408	-543
Balance on services	+190	+129	+174	+167
Net property income	+282	+174	+242	+416
Government spending	-239	-138	-283	-433
Net capital account	-165	-122	-192	-368
Deficit met by short-term money	109	270	467	761

the years of maximum deficit, however, all three of the major deficit items grew: the deficit on exports of goods; the increase in government overseas spending, nearly two thirds of which is military; and the net outflow of capital. Although the average annual increase of borrowing, at £110 million, may not seem large, the figures of nearly £300 million, nearly £500 million and finally nearly £800 million in the deficit years show the gathering seriousness of the crisis.

There are two parts to the problem. First, the worsening imbalance in export and import of goods, which in the three worst years accounts for more than half the total deficit. Second, the steady increase of short-term debt, by over £100 million every year. These are the two parts of the balance-of-payments crisis that faced the Labour government. The short-term loans could easily be withdrawn, and were in fact withdrawn at the first whisper of doubt about the possibility of maintaining the value of sterling in relation to other currencies. What could the government do?

Table 2 sets down the country's financial assets and liabilities side by side as they stood in December 1964. It will be seen that there was an overall positive balance, but the short-term balance was in deficit, even though, it must be remembered, this was after borrowing nearly £900 million from the International Monetary Fund. The government had another £470 million in its portfolio of securities, a large part of which could be - and was in the event - disposed of. But the short-term deficit

Table 2: UK financial assets and liabilities - December 1964

		Assests (£millions)		Liabilities (£millions)	
Long-term and short-term		15,725		14,160	Net: 1,565
Long-term:					
Inter-govt loans		505		1,850	
Other government		325		725	
Private investment		9,420		4,075	
of which: -Portfolio	3,600		1,500		
-Companies direct (excl. oil)	4,520		1,825		
-Oil companies	1,300		750		
Long-term total		10,250		6,650	Net: 3,600
Short-term:					
Trade credit		691		142	
Banking - sterling currency		1,165		4,631	
-non-sterling		1,626		1,856	
I.M.F. account		696		881	
Government portfolio		470		-	
Gold and reserves		827		-	
Short-term total		5,475		7,510	Net: -2,035

remained, and it only needed a swing from credit to debit of the traders, who buy and sell sterling from day to day for paying their bills, to start a further run on the pound. Much of the sterling currency debt of the London banks is held officially by foreign governments as reserves for their currencies; they were unlikely to try suddenly to change these from sterling into other currencies. But non-government holders would certainly try to get out of sterling in a major crisis.

The obvious course for the government would appear to have been to realize some of the long-term assets that had been built up overseas, and in this way to meet the short-term debt. But here there was a snag. These assets were largely in private bands. Moreover, two thirds were directly invested by companies, including the oil companies, in subsidiaries and branches overseas. Nevertheless, £3,600 million were in private portfolios, that is investments by persons and institutions in companies abroad. These could have been nationalized and sold to meet the debt. In fact discussions are now being held by the government with investment trusts with a view to persuading them to realize some of their overseas holdings and pass the dollars to the government. Such voluntary methods of realizing private assets abroad are very unlikely to be adequate. Yet it is clear that for the Labour government to have made compulsory purchases would have raised the whole question of the confidence of the City and of the foreign bankers.

Even if foreign exchange controls could have been imposed quickly enough and foreign assets could have been frozen, the process of government intervention could not have stopped there. The demand of the Left for nationalizing the private foreign portfolio would have required in effect nationalizing the whole banking system to prevent wholesale withdrawals of capital from Britain. Nor could intervention have been stopped at this point. Of course the withdrawal of capital takes no single piece of machinery or equipment with it, but the short-term effect on trade credit would have required government control over foreign trade as well.

There is an evident conflict here between the City's banking role and the needs of British industry. But this conflict lies in the whole structure of British capitalism. If the functions of the City of London were replaced by government control of foreign trade and finance, there would not only be a loss of some £250 million a year - the City's contribution from banking, insurance and other services to the balance of payments - but huge problems of restructuring would still face British industry. For it is the City bankers who finance industry both at home and in its operations overseas, and it is increasingly British industry itself that requires the outflow of capital each year that we have seen to be so large a part of the cause of the balance-of-payments deficits. To compete with their opposite numbers in the United States and West Germany, British firms have bad both to increase their hold on sources of oil and other industrial raw materials and to establish subsidiaries in their competitors' own markets overseas. The international company, as we have seen earlier, is the driving force of modern capitalism. To support its vast operations there must be a surplus in the balance of payments in the country from which it originates. Such a surplus can be found either from a direct surplus of the home country's exports over imports or from the repatriation of earnings from overseas operations; or, as we have just seen, from short-term borrowing. The very increase in the operations of overseas subsidiaries may tend to reduce direct exports by U.K. companies, and their earnings overseas may be required for reinvestment overseas. If this happens, short-term borrowing must increasingly be relied upon.

This is what has happened in Britain in the last fifteen years. But it would be missing an important aspect of the truth if we failed to recognize that the trick - the bankers' confidence trick of borrowing short and lending long - very nearly came off. If we combine the capital account and the property-income and government accounts in the balance of payments (that is by separating these from the private goods and services accounts) there really was a capital and income balance. But it was not large enough to pay for the military and other government overseas expenditure that such a balance involved.

Table 3 takes three periods since 1958 and sets down side by side the flows each way of income from property and investment, both from ploughing back of that income and from fresh capital (plus = flow into Britain; minus = flow out).

Table 3:

Flows	Year 1958 Income (£millions)	Investment	Average 1959-64 Income (£millions)	Investment	Average 1965-6 Income (£millions)	Investment
British Income from abroad and Investment going abroad	+684	-294	+739	-342	+970	-412
Foreign Income from Britain and Investment in Britain	-389	+104	-435	+195	-562	+212
Income and Investment balance	+295	-190	+304	-147	+408	-200
Government transfers	+3	-77	0	-107	0	-155
Military expenditure	+52	-173	+38	-224	+25	-295
Combined balance	-90		-136		-217	

The overall figures for investment include not only government loans to foreign countries but also the repayment by the government of foreign loans made to Britain. The suspension of repayments on the American loan, in 1965, accounts in part for the improved balance in the last two years. The other element in the apparent improvement was the sale by the government of some £200 million of its own portfolio of foreign investment in those years.

The fact must here be faced that even if overseas military expenditure had been sharply cut back by the government, it would have been necessary to increase the item of government transfers. For these are the grants made to ex-colonial lands, not only to replace their dependence on British military expenditure, as in Malta or Aden, but to help finance their economic development in such a way as to encourage them to go on buying British goods.

This analysis of the role of capital movements in the sterling crisis indicates the difficulties facing a government that was committed to remaining within the boundaries of capitalism. It also precisely illustrates the position of British capital. Since the war British capital investment has been built up overseas, not only in the old fields of oil and raw material extraction, but even more in the new field of manufacturing plants: mainly in the other advanced industrial lands and even in the U.S.A. By these means British capitalism tried to retain its dominating role. For many years, even after the war, the resources for its export of capital were found from the earnings of the colonial lands themselves, which by virtue of membership of the Sterling Area had to bank in London. The self-governing lands spent their own earnings, but the earnings of the colonies could be used to balance Britain's deficits. Now only Malaysia and the oil states remain to supply the resources for the City's long-term investments. Hence the wish to preserve the imperial role East of Suez at so great a cost. The cost of course is paid by the taxpayer; the benefits reaped by the investors.

Thus to preserve British capitalism and the imperial role, the government was forced to borrow again and again from the United States and other capitalist bankers. Devaluation of the pound in November 1967 marked the final downgrading of British capitalism from the first rank to at best the leader of the client states. The confidence trick could be maintained no longer. It is because some business men thought that a Tory government might have kept it up longer that anger has mounted against the Labour government. But the fundamental facts underlying the crisis of sterling are to be found in the inter-relationships between the banking role of the City and the decline of British industry.

31. The position of British industry

In 1950 British industry was not backward except in relation to the United States. British exporters still provided over a quarter of the manufactured exports of industrial lands, nearly as much as did the United States. By 1964 the British share had been halved, while U.S. and West German exporters were providing over 20 per cent each. In the decade after 1955, exports of British manufactures rose by about 3 per cent a year while imports of foreign manufactures rose annually by 9 per cent. The result was that, by 1967, manufactured imports into Britain were equal to three quarters of manufactured exports. Imports of machinery and transport equipment were equal to half the exports of these items, yet these were Britain's stock in Trade *par excellence*.

What had happened? It is not difficult to see, from the available figures, that investment in new equipment had proceeded faster on the Continent than in Britain. With productivity rising in U.K. manufacturing industry very much more slowly (by 37 per cent between 1955 and 1966) than elsewhere (50 per cent in the U.S. and 67 per cent in West Germany), increased wage costs per unit of output were pushing at British prices. Indeed, British firms, which export on average nearly a fifth of their output, had been forced to squeeze their profit margins in the export market. This can be seen from the fact that, whereas U.K. manufactured export prices rose by 27 per cent between 1955 and 1966 (well ahead of the figures for all other advanced industrial countries, around 15 per cent), this rise was much less than the rise over the same period in all home costs (36 per cent).

Not only were British manufactures becoming uncompetitive, but it was evident that British capital exports were failing to obtain similar rates of return to those of their competitors, at least to those of the U.S. In addition the rate of return on U.S. capital invested abroad was higher than on U.S. capital invested at home, while there was little difference in the two rates on U.K. capital. Indeed rates of return on British capital at home were declining steadily throughout the 1950s.

British industry was evidently caught in a pincers movement. U.S. and German firms were not only challenging the profits of British firms operating overseas; they were also challenging them in their own home market. United States firms were investing in their British subsidiaries throughout the 1950s at a rate of at least £100 million a year, and the resulting production was yielding a rate of return on capital twice as high as that enjoyed by British firms.

The power of United States capital depends, as we have seen earlier, on its enormous technological superiority. To compete in the world market any other producer requires lower levels of wages until his technology catches up. If his technology advances steadily, wages can rise. If his technology improves haltingly, and if productivity is stagnant or rises slowly, not only are wages threatened but so is the whole competitive position. And if only some producers in any country improve their technology, so that their higher productivity allows higher wages, but other industrial sectors or parts of the country lag behind, the tensions between different wage levels become serious. If this happens in a situation where there is in any case a tendency for imports to rise faster than exports, then wage increases in some sectors, plus credit released for electoral purposes, can easily push overall demand ahead of productivity and pull in huge waves of additional imports.

This brings us to a further problem facing British capitalism at the end of the 1950s. The power of British trade unions, in conditions of full employment, to raise wages ahead of productivity was important. In the late 1940s and early 1950s, real wages had undoubtedly lagged behind the rise in output per man. Profits had boomed. But from 1954 to 1960, hourly earnings in manufacturing industry in Britain, discounted for price increases - that is, then, real earnings - rose ahead of output per man-hour. Profits, as we have seen, were reduced. In West Germany and the U.S.A., by contrast, productivity rose faster than real earnings over these years. Profits in these two countries boomed, and investment in new plant and equipment leapt ahead.

The problem of rising earnings in relation to productivity was exacerbated for British industry by the nature of the Tory election booms in the 'never-had-it-so-good' 1950s. The share of the national income going into private consumption was raised in the booms at the expense of the public services. When the release of credit for private consumption had pulled in excessive imports and upset the balance of payments, a severe check was administered to all economic activity. The result was not only a stop-go cycle of current demand, but a series of checks to company investment plans. The share of the national product going to new investment was thus held back.

Just as growth is a cumulative process, so is decline. Once the British industrial base at home was weakened by the failure to invest a large enough proportion of the national product in new plant and equipment - and the Tory consumer booms can be held largely responsible for that - exports became less competitive, imports flowed in. When, at the same time, British capitalism was proceeding to build up its overseas operations and to support these with military bases, the strain on the balance of payments became serious. But each new check to growth while the balance was righted (after 1955, after 1960 and again after 1964) and each new wave of short-term borrowing from abroad at higher and higher interest rates only worsened the competitive position of industry. When demand is held back at home, investment in new plant stops. By contrast the surplus of exports from West Germany made possible continued growth. This created the opportunity for further investment in new plant, and so for still more competitive exports, until West Germany's payments surplus could easily finance the outflow of capital for the foreign operations of West German firms.

32. The response of British industry

There can be no doubt that 1960 marked a turning point for British capitalism. Until then British industry had been shielded by a combination of factors; the slow recovery of the defeated nations; the inflow of public and private capital including not only investments of U.S. firms but the dollar earnings of the colonies; the fall in import prices; the spending of war-time accumulations of reserves by the developing lands. At the same time the City of London had succeeded in moving very near to full sterling convertibility, and in re-establishing itself as the second, if not the first, financial centre of the world. Then the balance-of-payments crisis of 1960 revealed the fully exposed position of the British economy. West German exports of manufactures had surpassed those of Britain in 1958, while Japan and Italy were steadily increasing their shares. Partly as a result of the recovery of the defeated nations, world prices of food and raw materials were once more rising. The overseas countries of the Sterling Area were beginning to run deficits of their own to add to Britain's deficit. The 'Never-had-it-so-good' pre-election boom provided by the Macmillan government in 1959, when consumption increased ahead of output, only added the last straw.

The responses of British capitalism to this critical situation can be equally clearly dated from 1960. Some of these were deliberately planned. Most were the natural reactions of capitalists in a competitive situation. The two most obvious competitive reactions were the sudden increase in mergers and take-overs, and the renewed expansion of overseas investment by British companies. The result was that the largest companies in Britain achieved an even more dominating position in the economy than before.

The top 116 had by 1963 raised their share of all company assets to nearly 60 per cent of the total, and in the process had taken 90 per cent of the new capital raised in the previous seven years. The fastest growing third of the top 116 took nearly half of the new capital and almost doubled their share of the assets. If we include the giant oil and shipping companies, there is no doubt that the top 120 companies in Britain now own half of all assets, and probably account for nearly two thirds of all home sales. Fifty companies, including the oil and shipping companies, account for perhaps half the sales.

But despite these mergers and take-overs, even the giant British firms remained uncompetitive. For example, the seven top United States companies operating in Britain have a much larger share of income than of net assets. Indeed their income/assets ratio is about double that of the other large companies. British companies' net assets are not smaller on average in most industries (automobiles were the exception) than those of their United States counterparts. But their sales are very much smaller, since their sales/assets ratios in every field of industry are only about half those of the United States companies. The sales per employee are relatively lower still. In other words the technology of British companies is far behind that of the giant United States companies.

Consider then the implications of this great concentration of capital in the largest companies, when we see that they are also those that have become most internationalized. First, rather more than a fifth of annual net British company capital investment (i.e. excluding the investment of foreign company capital in Britain and excluding depreciation provisions) has in recent years been invested outside the country. This is a sum equal to the net annual investment of all the nationalized industries. In 1961 the net worth of overseas subsidiaries and branches was already equal to just under a fifth of the total net worth of all British companies.

Second, the result of this wave of overseas investment is that many of the largest British companies are selling nearly as much in foreign markets as at home, not mainly through direct exports but through their subsidiary companies. Indeed, the largest companies have come to rely on the medium and smaller companies to supply the exports for the balance of payments.

Why do the giant companies continue with their overseas investment, although the return to capital is no higher than at home?

The explanation is in our earlier analysis of the role of the international company in modern capitalism. Given the nature of the capitalist world market, and the lines of production into which industrial investment is attracted inside that market, there was nothing else they could do.

The respective *social* costs and benefits of £100 million invested at home or overseas are still hard to determine. The Reddaway Report raised serious doubts about the social return on overseas investment and even more on the balance-of-payments advantages, at least in the short run. Two things can be said with certainty. First, large British firms were bound to attempt to keep up in the capitalist market for private goods in the absence of government-planned international trade development. Second, £100 million invested at home will yield incomes that are more equally distributed than the dividends from overseas investment, and are more likely to be spent on home-produced goods and services than on imports.

33. Special characteristics of British capitalism

British capitalism differs in important respects from the pattern of development in the United States. There are in Britain, as in the U.S.A., giant corporations, with subsidiaries all over the world, deeply involved in government orders for arms and civil research. Outside their sales to the government, these giant companies rely on establishing by massive advertising campaigns a controlled market for long runs of innovated consumer products. Since Britain is a much smaller country, at a lower level of development, there are of course fewer really large companies here than in the U.S.A.: perhaps fifty to compare with the top 300 in the U.S.A.; or half a dozen with their top fifty which had assets of over $1 billion in 1965. But the differences go further than this:

1. The large U.K. company is technically less advanced than the large U.S. corporation and the gap has been widening;

2. as a result, U.K. company profits ratios (both to assets and to sales) are much lower and have been falling;

3. as a further result, large British companies have turned more and more to the government not only for military orders, but for wider government spending and recently for direct grants in aid;

4. with lower profits ratios the large U.K. companies have been forced to find more of their capital from the market than has been the practice of giant U.S. companies, at least when they operate in Britain.

Companies that have shown rapid growth in the U.K. have relied on external capital for about half of their finance. Only nine, out of the forty-two fastest growing in the top 116 companies in manufacturing and distribution with over £25 million assets, relied almost entirely on self-finance, and three of these were subsidiaries of the U.S. companies. Of the top seven U.S. companies, only Esso raised any sizeable amount of capital on the market. They did not, however, set aside a larger proportion of their annual income to reserve or depreciation than British companies. They simply achieved higher income/assets ratios and built their growth on this. About a third of the other large U.K. companies also relied very little on external finance, but although they had higher than average incomes/assets ratios they exhibited a very low rate of growth. We are evidently still a long way in Britain from the large self-financing American type corporation.

Nor does a study of the boards of directors of these top 116 companies reveal that they are mainly controlled by internal management. At least a third certainly are, but though these companies have higher income/assets ratios than the others and raise somewhat less capital in the market, they have displayed only an average growth rate. Their share of the net assets of the top 116 companies therefore did not rise, or barely rose, between 1957 and 1963. Moreover, most of the overseas-operating British companies, which were excluded from the 116 - companies like Shell, B.P., R.T.Z., P.&0. - are very obviously not controlled at the board level by inside managers. The role of industrial and financial controllers, who sit across a whole range of boards of industrial and financial companies, remains as important in Britain as ever.

Among these controllers the merchant bankers have lost none of their former importance. (See Table 4.)

Indeed in the process of rationalization, with mergers and take-overs at the very highest levels of British industry, the merchant bankers' role at home has grown. At the same time, the growing importance for the large British industrial companies of finding and controlling the funds for establishing and developing overseas subsidiaries has given merchant bankers a new lease of life in the field of capital exports. They are no longer concerned with raising capital in London for foreign governments and utilities, but they are deeply involved in the movements of sterling and foreign currencies earned abroad by the giant British companies.

Table 4: Merchant Bankers on Top Boards of Industry and Finance, 1958 and 1966

Type of board	Number of directorships		
	1958	1966	
Bank of England	4	3	(plus 2 ex-Governors)
'Big 8' banks	29	28	(all 8 banks)
Other banks	37	55	
Top 30 Insurance companies	73	49	(top 20 companies only)
Top 120 home Industrial companies	59	60	(45 different companies)
Top 30 overseas companies	39	43	
Totals	241	238	

The effectiveness of British capitalism, then, does not depend on a few giant corporations which dominate industry and government as in the U.S.A. but on the political unity and economic co-ordination achieved by its controllers. Here it is the C.B.I. Chairman and not the Chairman of British Motors who says 'what is good for the C.B.I. is good for the nation'. The power elite in Britain has an even stronger educational and social cohesion than Wright Mills described in the U.S.A. The movement of men between industry, finance and government, both as ministers and civil servants, is even more prevalent now in Britain than in the U.S.A. Such interlocking is more necessary to capitalism here: first, because the giant British companies are neither so dominant internationally, nor so independent financially; second, because for this and other reasons, they are far more dependent on state markets and state aid. This has a critical importance in understanding what has happened under a Labour government.

34. The role of the State

The response of British capitalism to the developments of the late 1950s was not limited to the reactions of individual firms in mergers, take-overs and overseas investment. Strong pressure began at the same time, from the Federation of British Industries, for tax concessions and grants towards investment. In this they were extraordinarily successful. While company income rose in current values from £3,700 million in 1956 to £5,000 million in 1964, U.K. taxes paid actually fell from £900 million a year to £800 million. Moreover, after years in which the very word 'planning' had been anathema in British business circles, and private consumption had cut steadily into public spending, the demand for state planning and state aid for industry was heard again.

There is plenty of evidence that it was the disastrous international performance of British industry revealed in the balance-of-payments crisis of 1960 that led to this demand. The three key F.B.I. pamphlets, *Civil Research Policy*, *Overseas Trade Policy* and *The Regional Problem*, all date from 1962. So does the demand for an incomes policy. All these policies specifically required increased state intervention to make British industry more competitive. 'Certain facts are operating to place limits on what private industry can do unaided', wrote the F.B.I. experts on civil research. 'The practice of other countries, notably the U.S.A., in assisting private industry in civil research and development gives them a strength which we must match or lose out.'

Table 5 traces the decline and recovery of state expenditure in the total national product between 1950 and 1964 and the continuation of the trend by the Labour government.

This shows the recovery and extension of the State's share, both of capital investment and non-military current expenditure. Despite the

increase in the number of old people in our population the share of benefits
in the national product has still not been raised again to the level achieved
in 1950. Expenditure on capital account - on roads and schools, colleges,
houses and hospitals - and current expenditure on their maintenance, are,
on the other hand, well beyond not only the low proportions of the
mid-1950s but of the first post-war Labour government too.

Table 5: share of State in G.N.P. as per cent

United Kingdom					United States
	1950	1955	1964	1966	1963
All state expenditure	41	38	43.5	46.5	29
Goods and services	22	19.75	27.5	28.75	21.5
- Military	7.75	8.75	6.5	6.75	9.5
- Other current	9.25	7.5	12.25	13	6
- Capital Investment	5.0	7.5	10.5*	10.5*	7.5
Payments to persons etc.	19	14.25	14.25	16.25	7.5
- Benefits	10	8	8.25	9	3.5
- Subsidies	4	2	1.75	1.75	2.0
- Debt interest	5	4.25	4.25	4.5	2

*In 1964 and 1966 Capital Investment includes 1.5 for loans to
companies and foreign governments.

The figures for capital investment and current expenditure on goods
and services by the State do not take into account the whole role of the
nationalized industries. These provide further extensions of state
intervention in the economy. The sales of the public corporations
amounted in 1964 to about £4,500 million, or just over a fifth of the total
for all industries including construction, transport and distribution. Their
share of gross capital formation also amounted to about 20 per cent of the
total, giving to the public sector as a whole, including central and local
government and nationalized industries, about a half of all investment.
Most of the equipment as well as current goods and services have of course
been bought by the public corporations from private business. Such
purchases provide for private industry an extremely important market,
which is largely risk-free and on which very high profits are often made (as
we are sometimes made aware in the case of defence contracts). Even more
important for private business, the public corporations have not only been
required to provide their goods and services at uncommercial prices (i.e.

below their economic cost) but have therefore been forced to borrow for their expansion at the rate of around £700 million a year. This they have done through the government from company savings in the private sector. Interest at 5 per cent on loans made to the public sector have thus provided an important addition to company income. Through this and other processes, the State now owns less than it owes: as Meade put it, 'so far as the net ownership of property is concerned, we live, not in a semi-socialist state, but in an anti-socialist state'.

Although the role of the State as a market both for goods and private capital has become crucial to British industry, two other recent developments are of almost equal importance. The first is the beginning of economic planning which has taken the form of consultation between industry, government and unions in the Economic Development Councils. George Brown's National Plan was in this matter an aberration and has been quietly buried. For the purpose of this planning, private industry has combined its forces under very powerful leadership in the C.B.I., and has shown every intention of using economic consultation to bring pressure to bear upon both government and unions. The remarkable result of the policies put forward by the F.B.I. for civil research, for overseas trade and for the regions is that government grants provided to private industry under a Labour government will reach in the year 1967-8 the staggering figure of £1,000 million with another £450 million in loans. Table 6 summarizes the figures under six headings.

Table 6: Government assistance to industry 1967-8

	Loans	Grants
	(£millions)	
1. Investment grants, tax allowances etc.	84	175
2. Selective and regional employment premium	-	235
3. Export rebates and credit	300	80
4. Research and development	-	245
5. Reconstruction and mergers	70	-
6. Agriculture, fisheries and forestry	-	275
Total	454	1,010

The estimated value of the output of industry in 1967-8 is 12,000 million, and of agriculture 1,100 million. Together the grants and loans are equivalent to over 10 per cent of the output. What is more important, these sums may be compared with the £2,000 million of depreciation provision made by companies annually, the £1,000 million put to reserve, and the £500 million raised in capital issued on the Stock Exchange. The State is today in effect finding finance for about a half of the *net* fixed capital formation of the company sector.

The second main development, closely connected with the first, has been the development of the concept of an incomes policy. Because of the rise in real earnings ahead of productivity, up to 1963, the control of incomes had become a major demand of British industry. George Brown, in a published correspondence with a merchant banker, Maxwell Stamp, in 1963, wrote:

> What we cannot do is to create the atmosphere in which people feel that the end product of their participation in a planned economy will be a basically unfair society. You cannot get an incomes policy accepted, to give you an example, in that atmosphere.

Brown's 'declaration of intent', that the aim of an incomes policy must be social justice, may be regarded as the creation of the right atmosphere. He had already assured his banking friend that though 'there may even be a fundamental disagreement between us about the kind of society we want to live in ... we could nevertheless quite obviously cooperate on planning the economy'.

Stamp had been worried that the necessary 'atmosphere' might mean 'that before we plan successfully for growth, we must remove or substantially reduce inequality'. He need not have worried. The Labour party's choice was being made the other way.

35. But what is the State?

The model now emerging can be seen with some clarity. It has been summed up, abstractly, and with an implication of inevitability, by Galbraith:

> The Government fixes prices and wages, regulates demand, supplies the decisive factor of production which is trained manpower, underwrites the technology and the markets for products of technical sophistication.

He went on to describe this as the 'convergence of the two ostensibly different industrial systems, one billed as socialism and that derived from capitalism'. But what we must then ask is the explosive question: who promotes this? Where does the dynamic come from, for the development of such a system? From society, or from capital?

It has been called the role of the State. But the actual composition of 'the State' is the key to any realistic answer. It was Adam Smith who spoke of 'the tacit, but constant and uniform, combination of masters not to raise the wages of labour', and he went on to observe that when the masters are challenged by 'combinations of servants, labourers and journeymen, [they] never cease to call aloud for the assistance of the civil magistrate'.

It was left for a later economist as Chairman of the first Prices and Incomes Board in Britain to argue that today it is the workers who 'could hold society to ransom. Here is supreme power no longer at the top but at the bottom'. How neutral then is the State?

The question is not whether the government provides a 'permanent executive committee of the bourgeoisie', although it may have looked like that during some Tory administrations. The question is whether the judges, the chiefs of police, the higher civil servants, the ambassadors, the heads of academies and other public institutions may be said in one way or another to be closely associated with the interests of private capital. Despite the recent rise of a certain middle-class meritocracy, there can be little doubt that the Establishment is still drawn from an extraordinarily narrow range of families, schools and colleges. The famous Tribunal which examined a leak of changes in bank rate in 1957, and the studies that followed publication of its evidence, revealed the close connexions of family and the association in school, college and club of the leading persons in government, civil service, judiciary, finance and business.

To identify these associations is not to suppose a conspiracy. What is really there is a common view about the way to work the institutions that have been built up in Britain during the period of capitalist development. It really makes little difference that much private capital is now managed by professionals on behalf of its owners, if the professionals themselves are drawn from the same class, are themselves property owners and share the same interest in advancing the power of capital over labour.

When Labour came to power it found (to quote the present Minister for Economic Affairs) 'a largely unreformed private sector whose personnel, at the board room level, was all too often recruited not on the basis of ability but on that of social and family connections'.

Again, it found civil servants who 'are not just administrators, coordinators and senior executives, as the constitutional text books would have it'; but who are 'permanent politicians' with 'a corpus of politico-economic doctrine - assumptions about the economy, about society, about Britain's role in the world' that will 'frustrate and blunt' the sharpest Ministerial cutting edge ... 'with the conventional wisdom of Whitehall'.

He could say that again.

36. Labour's aims and capitalist planning

The real role of the State was then already predicted. The Tory government and its civil servants were just becoming convinced of it when Labour was elected in 1964. What Labour found on entering office was a planning momentum of just that sort, with which the 'modernization' thesis could at once be associated.

The objects of British capitalist planning were increased efficiency, export competitiveness, profitability, and investment in growth; but also a break in the defences of traditionalist groups of workers and employers. Entry into the E.E.C. became an essential part of the programme, in order to bring outside pressure to bear on such groups. The other reason for British industry's support of entry into E.E.C. was the simple one, that 'if you can't beat them, you'd better join them'. Especially since 'they' were likely to absorb by association into their common market many of the countries of southern Europe and Africa which were major markets for British exports, for example Spain and Nigeria. Entry into E.E.C. was certainly not regarded as in any way incompatible with the kind of economic planning the C.B.I. was proposing, however incompatible it may have been with a possible Labour kind.

We have already noted George Brown's emphasis on creating the atmosphere (if not the reality) of greater equality and social justice. Combined with Mr Wilson's thesis on the urgent necessity of modernizing the economy, with the State taking the lead, the thinking of Labour leaders in fact fitted well with the momentum created by British industry after 1960. The 'fundamental disagreement' that Brown told his banking friend might exist 'between us about the kind of society we want to live in' could be buried in the obvious necessity to co-operate in planning the economy. A Labour government would carry through the further rationalization the economy needed, because it could manage the unions and offer some corrections to the anti-social working of market forces. A consensus of capital and labour could be achieved on the basis of some social reforms and a strengthening of the competitive position of British industry. While the Left hoped it could push the government leftwards, into more radical reforms, the Right believed it could keep the agenda firmly within the consensus by the facts of business pressure and the rigidity of existing political and economic structures.

Whether there was ever a middle way which combined the interests of capital and labour in a *national* plan, it is hard now to tell. What was bound to emerge was a compromise of some kind between the rival demands of capitalism and the unions. If economic growth could have been assured this would not have been difficult to reach. But with little or no growth, and even rising unemployment, the unions were bound to become increasingly defensive; their leaders increasingly alienated from the rank and file; employers increasingly suspicious that concessions would be made to growing trade union resistance. A Tory government could not have managed to control the unions even as far as the Labour Government has done. On the other hand, a Labour government inevitably finds difficulty in obtaining effective co-operation in rationalizing management. The middle ground of British politics always depended on the viability of British capital in a competitive world. As soon as this viability came into question the sharp alternatives of cuts at the expense of one side of industry or the other had to be faced. Before we conclude that the Labour government could have done nothing other than it did, we have to consider the possibility that in Mr Wilson's words it was 'blown off course' by events outside its control.

37. Labour and the crisis of the world economy

Indeed a major crisis was developing, for the first time since the war, in the whole capitalist world. Up to 1966 world production and world trade, at least in manufacturing, had grown at unprecedented rates: in the last eight years averaging in volume respectively 7 and 8 per cent a year. In such circumstances it was not difficult even for a backward British industry to increase exports at an average 4 per cent a year. By 1967 the main forces that had sustained this growth were becoming worked out.

There had been the increase in trade inside western Europe, engendered by the transfer of manpower from agriculture to industry and the internal exchange of goods within the European Economic Community. By 1967 the transfers of manpower and the tariff cuts which had produced this result were complete. Moreover, there had been the huge outflow of capital; both public and private, from the United States, associated with a great increase in overseas military spending. Since the surplus of United States exports over imports did not suffice to finance these flows, the United States began from 1958 onwards to run a steady balance-of-payments deficit of around $3 billion a year.

This was financed by sales of gold which reduced the stock of gold in Fort Knox by 1962 to the level it had been in 1929. Attempts were therefore made in 1962, as again in 1968, by the U.S. government to reduce its overseas spending and to repatriate more of U.S. private company overseas earnings. But the war in Vietnam once more raised the level of U.S. military spending overseas, and several countries, led by France, began to convert their dollar reserves into gold.

A crisis of liquidity, as the reserves of the great trading nations are called, then arose. Gold was still being produced at the rate of over $1 billion a year, but the possibility of gold being revalued in terms of the dollar led to nearly all new production in the capitalist world being offset by private hoarding. For a time Soviet and Chinese sales of gold to pay for imports of grain kept the gold reserves rising. Then in 1966 they actually began to fall for the first time since the war. The deficits on Britain's balance of payments in 1963, 1964, 1965 and 1966 provided some increase in available sterling. More important, an increase in 1965 of $2 billion in the reserve Quotas of the International Monetary Fund improved the situation for a time. The hard fact remained that, in 1967, world liquidity, which had been the equivalent of the value of over seven months of world trade movements in 1958, was down to the equivalent of only three months' trading. Without new forms of credit, trade was being strangled. And, equally serious, the primary-producing countries had hardly increased their reserves - the Sterling Area countries not at all - over their holdings in 1956. Reserves of the less developed countries were equivalent in 1967 to less than three months of their trading, and most of these reserves were held by just five comparatively small countries - Venezuela, Israel, Saudi Arabia, Malaysia and Thailand. But a third of Britain's trade is still with the Sterling Area countries and half of that with the less developed ones, of which only Malaysia and Kuwait count any reserves.

A very real danger arose in 1966 when the three greatest trading nations - the United States, Britain and West Germany - simultaneously began to pursue policies designed to reduce their own balance-of-payments deficits, without putting anything in the place of the finance these deficits had provided for other countries' trade. The danger was of a succession of beggar-my-neighbour policies of the kind experienced in 1931. The risk this time was not of competitive tariff-raising; this is now precluded by the General Agreement on Tariffs and Trade. The risk was and is (very markedly in 1968) of a series of beggar-my-neighbour deflationary policies, combined here and there with devaluation. If several large countries try to balance their payments by increasing their exports and reducing their imports through deflationary measures, the net result is almost bound to be a general reduction in the trade of all of them and thus in the trade of all other countries. This is what happened in 1931 and it can happen again.

How far was realization of this danger the reason for the Labour government's vacillating attempts between 1964 and 1967 to avoid either sharp deflation or devaluation? Were there no alternatives open to the government when it came to power and was faced by a balance of payments deficit of some £800 million?

38. The Rake's Progress

Harold Wilson in opposition had always argued that Tory stop-go and all that it implied could be avoided by the use of physical controls: the steering wheel in place of the alternation of brake and accelerator. 'Ruthless discrimination will be practised', he promised in the Spring of 1964, so that 'growth should not be stopped when imports threatened to rise too fast.... Essential industries will be encouraged, those of lower priority will be held back'. The 1964 Labour election manifesto proposed long-term trade agreements with Commonwealth countries to build stability into our foreign trade. The 1966 election manifesto argued for a 'concerted world effort ... to enable overseas countries to earn the foreign exchange essential for their development programmes ... international commodity agreements and arrangements for finance for increasing and stabilising the export earnings of primary producing countries'.

Wilson himself had spoken at the 1963 Labour Party Conference on 'Labour and the Scientific Revolution' in the following terms:

> The stop-go economy of the last 12 years failed because the expansionary phases had not created growth in those industries which could provide a permanent breakthrough in Britain's export trade or a lasting saving in imports. . . . Monetary planning is not enough. What are needed are structural changes in British industry and we are not going to achieve those on the basis of pre-election spurts every four years in our industry, or on the hope of selling the overspill of the affluent society in the highly developed markets of Western Europe. What we need are new industries and it will be the job of the next Government to see that we get them.... When we set up new industries based on science there need be no argument about location, on costly

        bribes to private enterprise to go here rather than there. We
        shall provide the enterprise and we shall decide where it goes.

What happened? Almost immediately after the election, we had
Wilson's commitment, at a Mansion House banquet in the City of London,
that 'sterling would be kept riding high'. Devaluation was ruled out, but
where now was the promised alternative to deflation and 'stop-go'
stagnation? In fact, by 1964, the size of the payments deficit would have
required physical controls on imports, on foreign exchange movements and
on building and investment at home. But the crisis in the balance of
payments was due also to heavy overseas military expenditure, and to a
huge outflow of capital in the months before Labour took office. And these
were in turn related to the requirements of an international economic
political and military system which imposed constraints on Britain's
freedom to act. To deal with the problems of debt and deficit in any radical
way would have involved an immediate confrontation, not only with this
international system but also with those elements of it - the British financial
institutions and large firms, themselves integrated, as we have seen -
through which, to modernize the economy, Labour intended to act. The
very institutions that would be forced to give up their private interests to
the will of an elected government were the only institutions through which
the economy could be managed; unless, of course, socialist institutions
were created to replace them. And it was just this option of the creation of
socialist institutions which the Labour leadership had given up in advance.
What was intended as a working compromise became first a constraint and
finally a capitulation. The elected government could direct and manage
everyone and everything else, but not capital.

The immediate form of the payments crisis was an increasing
imbalance between exports and imports particularly in manufactured
goods. In fact, the system of international division of labour in the
advanced capitalist world means that the import of manufactured goods is
always growing. On top of this, British industry was no longer fully
competitive with the newer industries on the continent of Europe and in
Japan, and this, ironically, was due to a failure of investment because of the
stop-go policies imposed as a reaction to previous balance-of-payments

crises. Devaluation would have corrected the immediate competitive situation. But those on the Left who advocated devaluation did so as part of a package of proposals for direct physical intervention in the economy by the government.

In the event the government in 1964 neither devalued nor deflated. The import surcharge of 15 per cent in 1964, reduced to 10 per cent in 1965, and abolished in 1966, was no alternative to devaluation. It was designed to reduce imports but did nothing to expand exports. A small increase in interest rates, an attempt at income restraint, and a massive loan took the place of deflation, until this was finally forced on Labour, in the crisis of July 1966. Labour's commitments to increase pensions, remove health charges and expand school building and public-sector housing had been partly fulfilled. But no corresponding cuts were made in the private sector and among the rich. The inevitable result was that, with fully utilized resources, and only a very modest increase in productivity from investment in the last years of Tory rule, imports were pulled in faster than exports could rise, and round the whirlpool we went yet again.

The deflationary measures of July 1966 were designed to cut back *all* spending by a credit squeeze and a stop on wages. But the government was caught once more, as previous Tory governments had been, by the fact that the very measures taken to deflate - increased interest rates and taxes on consumption - only served to raise prices. Moreover, reduced sales in the home market raised unit costs and checked the investment plans of firms trying to expand in export markets. It was clear that exports were failing to catch up with imports. The gap between them widened steadily in the last quarter of 1966 and the first half of 1967. This was *before* the Suez closure and the dock strikes.

The mistake in this second phase of Labour's policies lay in supposing that it is possible to increase efficiency with programmes which retard overall growth. The attempt to sustain investment in the regions of high unemployment while holding back growth elsewhere could never succeed. Firms that don't intend to increase their capacity anyway, because of the depressed market, are not going to invest anywhere despite the extra grants - the 'bribes' in 1963 phraseology - offered for the 'black' regions. All that the grants do is to provide private industry with a gift for doing what it would have done anyway. And what it will not do is then not done by anyone; a 'Labour' government does not do it, on its own account, because it has put business 'confidence' above national efficiency.

A second and far more serious set of mistakes was to suppose that it was possible to reconcile the needs of the low-paid and the pensioners with so-called incentives to management and private capital; to reconcile the growth of the public sector with avoidance of cuts in the private sector; and to reconcile economic growth for raising living standards at home with the preservation of the pound as a world currency and the City of London as its custodian. To pursue any one set of these policies realistically means rejecting the other set. It is this fact of choice that has been persistently hidden by the idea of a political consensus - the lion and the lamb, the capitalists and the unions, the City and the poor - in an undifferentiated 'New Britain'.

Of course the facts intervened. In the winter of 1967 unemployment was running at above 3 per cent for men and at 2.4 per cent overall. The public sector which had played a crucial part in the relatively expansive and progressive phase of British new capitalism was being rapidly run down and out. In 1960 employment for men in coal, on the railways, in gas, water, and electricity undertakings and in the steel industry amounted to $11\frac{1}{2}$ per cent of all male employment. By 1964 this had been reduced to just over 10 per cent and after three years of Labour government to less than 9 per cent. By 1971 it will have fallen to $7\frac{1}{2}$ per cent, given current proposals for reducing the mining industry and rationalizing steel. This melting away of the public sector meant a return to the old callous pre-war labour and manning policy in key sectors of the economy. The long losses of the wage freeze and of rising prices combined with these other factors to make it inevitable that the government's policies for rationalization and 'spare capacity' were bitterly resisted.

The resistance led to strikes, in the docks and elsewhere, which were of course very damaging to the economy and which provoked a new general crisis. But these strikes were not accidents, the results of being 'blown off course'. They were the inevitable result of the real economic policy being followed. Only policies which actually provided new jobs, more equality, and more control over the conditions of their working lives could have won the co-operation of the workers whose livelihood was being threatened. But the government was creating fewer jobs, more inequality and less union control over conditions of work. Which side they were on is clear from the fact that all major conflicts, since 1964, have been between the government and the unions, and not between the government and the employers, or the government and the City.

So the British economy failed to grow. Production was stagnant, but imports were continuing to rise. No alternative trading arrangements had been made with trading partners in the Commonwealth or Eastern Europe, who were planning their economies and could have entered constructive trade agreements. Devaluation was finally the only 'option' left.

39. Devaluation and after

Devaluation by itself solves nothing. It provides the opportunity for a solution, or rather for different solutions, of Britain's crisis. Combined with physical controls over the home market and over foreign-exchange movements, it could have been used by the Labour government at any time since November 1964 to prepare the way for a socialist solution. Three years later it is being combined with deflation and savage cuts in public spending in a further attempt at a capitalist solution.

Since devaluation means that the prices of our imports rise, as well as the prices of our exports falling, in terms of foreign currencies, it is evidently on the balance between the two effects that devaluation will be judged by any person or by any company. For most exporters a 15-per-cent devaluation means that costs can be expected to rise by only about 5 per cent (or 7 per cent including the loss of the export rebate), so that they should be able to cut their foreign prices by up to 8 per cent. Whether they do this or not will depend on how much extra they can hope to sell by lowering prices. British exporters have had their prices squeezed in foreign markets recently, and many have probably been making little or no profit on their exports. They may be expected to raise their profit margins now, but the 8-per-cent improvement in their competitive position, in some cases, only puts them back where they were in 1963. Productivity in West Germany, for example, has risen over 8 per cent faster than it has in Britain. And since growth in the world market is slowing down, every increase in the sales of British firms must from now on be almost entirely at the expense of foreign firms.

Consensus politics, we argued earlier, were only possible in a viable British economy working within an expanding capitalist world market. They were undermined by the failing strength of the British economy; a crisis of the world market would deliver the *coup de grâce*. What then are the real prospects?

If new plans are quickly put into operation for increasing world liquidity, and world trade maintains its expansion, and if exactly the right balance is found between home and foreign demand for British industry to expand at minimum unit costs, with minimal labour troubles, then exports will probably rise rapidly and a large surplus will be established on the balance of payments at least by 1969. A home-based boom could follow in 1970, 'in time for the next election'. But even in these most favourable conditions, the result will be a very sharp change in the division of the national product between capital and labour. Profits will boom while real earnings will be held back by the rising price of imported foods. Higher food prices and cuts in public spending, predicated to allow for increased exports, are already hitting particularly hard at pensioners and low-paid workers.

But these most 'favourable' assumptions, which are being widely made by orthodox economists, are based on most uncertain foundations. New plans for increased world liquidity are in abeyance until the U.S. government, by its measures of January 1968, reduces its payments deficit: a reduction which in itself will worsen the liquidity position. Gold might still be revalued if the deficit is not reduced. Although this would increase world liquid reserves it would not help Britain, which has no gold; and the competitive revaluations that followed might leave Britain where she had been before November 1967. Even if nothing more serious happens in the next year or so, the devaluation of the pound has greatly weakened the purchasing power of all the other Sterling Area countries. The value of their reserves is reduced, and they may have much more difficulty than British industry in benefiting by extra sales for their primary products in world markets. This especially applies to the less developed countries which have been important markets for British exports.

The assumption that the balance of home and foreign demand can be got just right is more doubtful even than the assumption about the growth of the world market. The only measures which the government is allowing itself to use to reduce home demand, in order to make room for meeting new export orders, all cut into wages and into the needs of the poor, while leaving capital and the demands of the rich almost unscathed. Yet these measures - cutting government expenditure on the social services and restraining wages - are the only weapons in the government's armoury while it refuses to use discriminatory physical controls. In the past, income restraint was not at any point used to discriminate in favour even of the lowest-paid workers. As the government now introduces what is called 'selectivity' in the social services, its point is not to give greater help to the poorest but to cut the whole bill without the poorest suffering any *extra* loss. This has always been the objection of socialists to 'selectivity' - rent rebate schemes, payment for prescriptions, etc.: that it is an excuse for general cuts in the public services and inevitably leads to the re-emergence of two services, one for the poor and one for the rich.

Continuing wage restraint and cuts in social services might just be tolerated a little longer, if production for export began at once to take up the slack. No one, however, believes that this will happen quickly. The cuts come first and the export-led expansion is to follow. Some increases in output at home may soon occur, if only to replace higher-cost imports, but there is still the ugly prospect of a high level of unemployment for many months. This is partly because of the rapid rundown that is planned for manpower in at least three industries: steel, coal and railways. The last two of these are particularly labour-intensive, and coal is in regions where without special government intervention there will be no export industries or import-substituting industries.

If unemployment, at least in the 'black' regions, is added to restrained wages and social service cuts, a major collision of government and labour is inevitable. If general unemployment can be held down, the government might get by with a continuation of only the minor battles that have marked its 'progress' since taking office. It could take on the miners and the steel workers separately as it has taken on and contained, in turn, the seamen, the dockers, the busmen, the railwaymen. It can hardly hope, however, to avoid a still further straining of loyalties and a still further extension of the anger and sense of betrayal that are now vivid in the labour movement.

Conditions are then unlikely to be favourable for the co-operation between unions, government and employers in the massive redeployment and retraining which real modernization and rationalization would imply. Whatever agreements are reached at the top will be challenged from below, if the fear of unemployment is strong, and if the threat of a wider margin of 'spare' capacity is fulfilled. It is hard to believe that, without using physical controls, the government could manage a deteriorating situation after devaluation in any other way than by the most ruthless capitalist measures. The unions would have to be divided and their power broken. The Left would be finally alienated from the government and the basis for a new kind of coalition government would exist. What can still save the Labour government, as it now exists, is only the revival of world trade and a series of lucky strokes (not strikes!) in getting the balance of home and foreign demand exactly right at every stage.

40. The power of capital and labour in Britain

Whether Britain's devaluation is a success in capitalist terms, or a failure and has to be repeated, the challenge to labour is still desperately serious. It is not enough for the Left to complain of consensus politics and to show where they have led. Nor can the Left limit itself to cheering on the isolated movements of resistance of some militant workers. It must develop and publicize measures which will unite the demands of all workers for the right to work and for a better living: a demand that is felt far more widely than in a few critically militant sectors. This unity may have to be built from below, but it would be the ultimate in sectarianism to neglect the strengths that still remain in the trade unions and the Labour party as agencies of change. It must be the task of predominantly intellectual groups like the New Left to make the analysis and discover the programmes that will unite every socialist in the labour movement with the organized workers throughout industry.

And then the greatest mistake we could make would be to suppose that capitalism in Britain is stronger than it is, or that labour is weaker. We can examine certain weaknesses of British capital that labour should exploit. There is, first, the potential conflict between financial and industrial interests. This has been reconciled only by policies of overseas expansion which suited both the City and the larger industrial companies. Devaluation is the beginning of the end of the role of sterling as a reserve currency and as a medium of world trade exchanges. The power of the City bankers is bound to be challenged, whether by the increasing development of self-finance at home and abroad, among the giant companies, or by the growth of state intervention in foreign trade. Divisions between the City and industry are bound to grow as the British economy tries to adjust more and more to a Swedish rather than a United States model.

There are other capitalist divisions to be exploited, on behalf of the working people and the true future of Britain. First, there is the division between British- and American-owned firms. This extends far beyond the borders of Britain and includes the whole field of patents, licences and manufacturing rights. Secondly, there is the division between the large and small companies. The interests of the latter cannot be entirely neglected by the leaders of the C.B.I., since the effectiveness of British capital is, as we have seen, more dependent on its unity than on its giants. Thirdly, there is the division of interest between those companies which are primarily interested in expanding their sales at home and by exports and those which are more concerned with establishing overseas subsidiaries either to maintain their overseas markets or to control their sources of supply from overseas.

It is one of the most startling facts that we have disclosed in the British economy that although the top fifty companies account for nearly half home sales, they provide less than a quarter of all exports. So long as the smaller companies go on exporting enough goods in relation to imports, there will be a balance in foreign payments to allow the large companies to export capital for their operations overseas. If imports rise too fast then growth at home must be checked. In this process not only is the whole economy held back and unemployment allowed to rise, but the smaller companies, dependent for profits on maintaining their sales, and for finance on trade and bank credit, are hit harder than the large companies with their semi-monopolistic positions and their internal reserves of funds. This is not to suggest the possibility of winning the support of a 'national capitalism' for socialist policies, but there is a real possibility of keeping certain groups of British industry effectively neutral in the continuing and major struggle with United States capital.

One further division in existing capitalist industry should not be overlooked. This is the frustration and irritation of the technologists who find not only very much less advanced fields of work in British industry compared, for example, with U.S. industry, but also very much less scope for their personal development, in the tradition-bound cousinhood of British finance and industry, than in the more open and pioneering climate of U.S. business. The brain drain is not only a serious problem for the national economy; it is a major irritant inside British industry.

When we turn to examine the strength of Labour in Britain today, we have to note several major factors in the trade union movement in Britain:

1. Despite the decline of industries where trade union membership was very large, such as the coal mines, railways, and textiles, the total number of unionists has increased and the organized proportion of the total manual work force has been maintained.

2. Despite the difficulties of organizing white-collar workers in unions, there has been a great increase in recruitment among such workers and the unity of manual and non-manual workers has been growing.

3. Despite the massive attack by press and radio on shop stewards, work-place bargaining and shop-floor militancy, the trend has been not so much for local movements to be contained within national bargains as for the T.U.C. to be forced into more militant positions. See its evidence to the Royal Commission, and the critical Congress resolution, in 1967, on overall economic policy.

4. It is not just in more advanced sectors like the motor industry, or in areas of traditional labour solidarity, that strong union actions, official and unofficial, have been taken. There has been widespread resistance to government economic policy and the threat of legislation. This has not only been negative resistance. As it must be to succeed, it is becoming positive, as notably in the comprehensive group of alternative policies now being pressed by the Transport and General Workers' Union.

These are the real terms in which the struggle between labour and capital goes on. It seems at times unequal, and there is considerable confusion. But it is a struggle that is not yet over by any means. On the contrary, in the full scale of the crisis now opening, it is certain, sooner or later, to move into a new and critical phase.

41. There are alternative policies

Our concern, as socialists, is with the needs and aspirations of the working people. These needs have disclosed themselves, with a bitter clarity, at every point of our analysis. The need to gain control over the productive process and over real wealth is the same need as that for the extended care of people, in work, education and housing, or in age, sickness and disability. It is the assertion of different priorities, against the internal and limited priorities of capitalism. Only when there is democratic control, over the whole processes of production and investment, can a human distribution be steadily achieved.

This is then the first policy we have learned: that actual human needs, in our real social conditions, cannot be set against the needs of production, as a marginal or residual claim. The continual frustration of these needs, by what are called the realities of debt or modernization, is in fact, as we have shown, the political acceptance of the internal priorities of profit in modern productive conditions. And then it is not only that human needs are dragged at the tail of this aggressive organized capitalism. It is that the usual formulation, that British people must go on being in need so as to make Britain strong, is an evident lie, in that the priorities are not even those of our own country's capitalism, but of an international system, economic, political and military, which in its own internal logic is continually overriding national interests.

It is certainly necessary to make Britain strong, and this is not just some selfish national aim. When we are asked to yield priority, to some international claim, we must always ask: what internationalism? There are indeed urgent claims on us, from the poor two thirds of the world, which we are bound to meet. But we shall only be able to do this if we refuse the priorities of that other internationalism: the overriding of all other interests for the creation of a market in which the giant international companies can operate. The true source of the poverty of most of Africa, Asia and Latin America is, as we have shown, the taking of priority by this same market and its supporting political institutions. In intervening in our own economy, to refuse the priorities of the international companies and bankers (including of course those that are based in Britain) we would be acting in a national interest which corresponds with the needs of the poor nations. From either point of view, this duty is now very urgent.

What would this mean, in practice? We have already seen that it is possible to respond, strongly, to what has been the main weakness of the economy, by nationalizing British privately-held foreign shares and securities. But this implies, as we have shown, extensive intervention in the banking system and in the capital market, and also, if this is to be more than a negative control, the creation of new institutions to make national decisions on production and investment. In the very exposed position of Britain's international trade, it implies also positive government action to meet the real need which has caused the major companies to export capital: the competitive international situation. Only national trading agreements, with the developing lands, with Eastern Europe and with others whose economies are subject to economic planning, can provide an alternative to the external priorities of the present system. It is in this context, but also as an immediate defence against those external priorities, that import quotas would be established, and a total control instituted over foreign exchange. The role of sterling as an international currency would be steadily cut back: first, by lowering bank rate and refusing the deposits of 'hot money' whose movements consistently interfere with our economy; second, by putting the pound on a floating exchange rate, between wider fixed points.

The intervention in the banking system, already foreseen for international reasons, would be extended, in itself and in the insurance companies, as a way of gaining national control over our real national sources of investment. This control would be linked with the production institutions already outlined, for developing resources at home and for fulfilling export contracts. There would need also to be a major tax on private wealth. The money gained in these ways for investment would not be handed out again in the existing kinds of grants for private industry, but would be used to establish new science-based enterprises in new forms of social ownership.

The correct response, for example, to the decline of the mining industry is not the present policy of accepting the priorities of the international oil companies, both in fuel oil and in their stake in what should be our national resources of North Sea gas, and then leaving the colliery areas to a process of persuading private firms to set up there on grants. It should be, first, a clear reworking of real costs in fuel: not just the immediate costs, at the point of market delivery; but also the consequent costs, in a financial system dominated by institutions based outside Britain; in the military and political support, now so expensive to Britain, on which those international firms, and especially the oil companies, now rely; and in the consequences, at every level from transport to housing, of the social dislocation and distortion of an economy planned only in the companies' interests. It should be, second, and on the basis of this reworking, a policy of new direct investment in the declining areas, by forms of ownership which could include the participation of trade unions, local authorities and co-operative societies; a greatly extended and publicly directed retraining scheme, locally based and with greatly improved allowances; and a following through, in related areas such as fuel distribution, and, as now partly proposed, in transport, of the same social priorities. This kind of response, which would be effectively in the Labour tradition; would be the pilot experiment for new policies and institutions in the existing growth areas, for it would be wrong to confine a socialist policy to the poorer regions, repeating the error of the existing public enterprises.

This range of socialist policies of course involves controls, but this is simply, as we have always argued, the building of public controls to replace the private controls which, though in new and complicated ways, now effectively determine the lives of the majority. That common current experience in Britain, in which what is obviously needed seems always to be deflected and decided on some other grounds, is not just the result of a very complicated society; it is mainly the result of the hidden logic of the capitalist and financial institutions we have described, and of their supporting system, in the State and corporate bureaucracy. Thus the siting of a third London airport at Stansted is not a social decision, but runs back, directly, to the relative costs deriving from a system of military airfields. Everywhere, now, we are faced with what looks like a realistic, practical accounting, even when it somehow produces the selling of carrots from Texas in the middle of an English horticultural region. The reason is that the accounting follows the internal convenience of the system, and pushes all consequent costs off to another, apparently irrelevant account. It is this that must be challenged, over the whole range.

It will be necessary, for example, to review the costing we have been offered on British agricultural production; a costing which can be used, in its local ways, to discourage this real national investment, itself so closely related to the present precarious balance of imports and exports. There is scope for further long-term international agreements, directly between food imports and manufactured exports: these will only materialize, on mutually acceptable terms, by government decisions, rather than by the free play of the existing indirect market. But the opportunity to increase, in major ways, British home agricultural production (as could be done, in the first stage, by some £200 million) should undoubtedly be taken, in a full context of relevant costs. In the same way, decisions in such matters as shipbuilding should no longer be left to private companies, on the basis of point-of-sale costs, but should be regularly translated into real costs, including foreign currency and the cost of unemployment in our own shipyards.

One major way of ensuring real social controls is the increasing intervention of the organized working-class movement, in its own right rather than indirectly through a political party. The existing corporate bureaucracy, of the State and private industry, is capable of commanding any new institutions and policies, and turning them to its own purposes, unless there is real countervailing power. It is not enough for the trade unions to dig in and resist change. To survive at all, in their original values, they will have to raise the costs of their co-operation, which is still vital. This means, first, the continuing extension of workers' control over such matters as safety, dismissals, and discipline. But it means, also, a more positive intervention in central economic decisions. 'Opening the books' is at the centre of this claim. Trade unions, either nationally or locally, will see the increasing need of refusing any kind of decisive agreement, whether in productivity, wages or manning policies, unless it is on the basis of the full disclosure of all relevant accounts, and an accompanying study of social as well as local industrial costs. A socialist trade-union policy envisages a step-by-step extension of workers' control to the point where it engages with the policies emerging from the wider democratic process, at which point the power of capital can be isolated and ended.

This two-way process is now very important, for it is in just the separation of producers and consumers, of industries and communities, of internal accounting and social accounting, that capitalism has done its greatest damage. For the proper defence and improvement of their working conditions, the trade unions cannot afford to isolate themselves in their separated function as producers, from all the other aspects of their own and their neighbours' lives. The capitalistic tactic, now, is to bring about this isolation, and then either to buy it off, in favourable situations, or to build resentment against it, in situations where they do not want to pay. Workers' control is an important form of immediate local democracy, but it must also, by continual extension and connexion, be seen as a part of a general democratic process.

Thus we support not only the immediate demands of unions in particular industries, but also such far-sighted and general policies as the campaign for a minimum wage, which would have critical effects on the whole pattern of social security. The needs disclosed in our social analysis, in social security, in housing, in education and in health, depend on this kind of linking. They are the result of the investment decisions we described, reducing this essential public sector to so low a level. These decisions can only be reversed, and a proper social expenditure be restarted, if there is the means of intervention at the very early point when total investment decisions are being taken.

Thus what we find we need, against the priorities of capitalism, is a socialist national plan. This will be very difficult to draw up, in the necessary detail, but it is because this was not done, by the Left, in the fifties and sixties that we got first a capitalist national plan and then the naked return of market priorities. The trade unions and the campaigners in social security, housing, health and education, together with socialist economists, could begin, from now, laying the foundations for this: as a building of necessary immediate demands into a general programme.

These are national duties, but it follows from our whole analysis that they will have to be undertaken in an international context, in which our position is already gravely weakened. Certainly, in an economic programme, it is necessary to halt and push back the penetration of our economy by United States capital: the perpetual investors, like the property speculators in our cities, who come always with readily available money, which seems a welcome alternative to the difficult business of raising money of our own, but which of course is only being brought to make a profit out of us, and is far more expensive in the end. To overcome their real advantage, in size and technological superiority, will be an immense fight, in which we are bound to seek allies, in wider trade associations and through specially planned joint-development projects, not just in western Europe (where the existing political forms reflect the same priorities of the international companies) but in the advanced socialist economies.

This is our very urgent interest, yet we find set against it, not merely a set of economic and financial institutions, but a whole political system. Drifting towards the ignominy of a client capitalism, we have seen the extensive development of a client politics, a client militarism, and a client culture. As the old class marks of a dominating Britain fade, this client apparatus, extensively established in every field, and with most of the national communications system safely in its hands, confronts us as an enemy who is very difficult to recognize because his accents and appearance are English, though his decisive agency runs back to the corporate power of the United States. There are many ways in which this apparatus can be resisted, day by day. But the organizing way, to which all others can be related, is resistance to the invading priorities of the most extreme development of the system, in military expenditure and in actual war. There have been some cuts, in future military spending, but by the end of the decade this will still be (at 1964 prices) more than £1,860 million. There is an imperative need for further drastic reductions, and this economic interest discloses itself as a political necessity, to break the stranglehold of a whole system.

Thus, in international policy, we must continue the existing commitments of the Left: to stop U.S. aggression in Vietnam; to prevent the betrayal of southern Africa to a connecting racialism and imperialism; to give up Britain's expenditure on nuclear weapons, and withdraw from an overall nuclear strategy. We must also assume new duties with more vigour. We have a particular duty to reject, on every occasion, the official descriptions of international reality. As access to the central media of communication becomes more difficult, so it becomes more important that socialists should take more systematic steps to maintain international communications of their own, and to pass their information on in every possible way. The very general boycott in the British media of the hearings of the International War Crimes Tribunal in Stockholm and Copenhagen (in 1967) underlines this point.

The details of foreign policy must be contested week by week, as they arise. But the perspectives are clear. In Europe we must press for disengagement between East and West in the political sphere (whether in the form of nuclear-free zones and a European Security Pact, or in piecemeal initiatives by individual nations), and for active association in economic, cultural and social spheres. However the question of the 'Common Market' is resolved, we must not lose sight of our priorities. Europe, including western Europe, is more than a market, and the decisive questions are not at that level. It is essential that we co-operate, at every stage, in the necessary process of political change in Europe, with the single objective of ending the outdated policies of the Cold War. This obliges us to oppose the capitalist alliance of NATO and its open and covert political aims; to resist the promotion by the United States of West Germany as a military and nuclear power; and to prevent any hardening of economic structures which would divide Europe and harm the rest of the world.

Such priorities are continuous with our necessary role in Asia, Africa and the Middle East. It is imperative for Britain to disengage from its position as junior partner - allotted its role and zones - in United States international policy. While we cannot foster illusions as to its past or present role, we should support any attempts to reclaim the United Nations as an effective agent in peace-making and in international aid. The convulsions of Asia and Africa, in our view, are a necessary process of political and social change, in which our weight must be thrown on the side of the hungry and the poor. As part of this change, we must redefine aid in a new strategy of co-operative development, for we cannot withdraw ourselves selfishly from the world crisis of poverty and population growth. The problem of development must be taken out of the context of capitalist trading relations, and this involves as much change in our own society as in the newly emerging countries.

In all these changes of policy, our relationship with the United States must cease to be a decisive factor. Our practical dependence on the United States, expressed in political and military alliances, confirmed by various forms of economic penetration, and supported, as a planned operation, by many kinds of cultural and educational colonization, makes any attempt at disengagement a fight from the beginning. We would not wish in such a fight, to rely on the counter-force of crude nationalism. We have noted with encouragement the emergence in the past few years, on the campuses and in the squares of the great cities of the United States, of a movement for peace and against imperialism, which works towards the same internationalist objectives as our own. The *élan* and courage of this growing movement of the American people presents an urgent claim upon us for our solidarity.

What we have to disengage from is a complex political system. We can only do this intelligently if we begin by opposing the British political and economic system which is making the subordination inevitable, and, as part of this change, by making new international contacts. What we are committing ourselves to is an international political struggle which includes the important political struggle within the United States. We shall work for the withdrawal of United States troops and bases from Britain and its associated territories, and this, though necessary and urgent, is not a merely negative policy, but a deliberate initiative against an international political system which depends on bases and client states.

In the continuing struggle against imperialism in Asia, Africa, and Latin America (or, as in Greece, in Europe), what is evident is that the

changing conditions demand a quite new quality of alert response from
British socialists: first, because a successful revolutionary movement - in
Brazil or India, Bolivia or Cambodia - might at once threaten the world
equilibrium of power, and thus provoke crisis: second, because immediate
responses of solidarity may be called for which cannot be prescribed within
the old formulas of 'pro'- or 'anti'-Soviet movements.

We must distinguish three types of this response. In the first,
solidarity is a wish to defend these societies and movements against any
external aggression, without either assent to or dissent from their forms and
ideologies. In the second, we express a general historical assent to these
forms, while reserving the right to criticize, in the most fundamental way,
their particular features. In the third, where solidarity is confused with
apologetics, there is an emotional identification (with China or Russia or
Cuba) which is so strong that not only are all features of those societies
assented to (and sometimes exactly those features which, next month or
next year, the ruling group in these countries themselves denounce) but
also imitative forms and an imitative ideology are imported into the British
movement.

The first approach seems to us plainly inadequate; the third approach
can be, and has often been, damaging; and it has frequently been
ridiculous. Our own approach is the second; and within it there is room for
many differences of emphasis. In fact such differences exist among us in
the appreciation and criticism of communist movements. But what is
evident is that in the past decade the volume of criticism *within* the world
communist movement has grown and diversified, and it is likely to
continue to grow if and in so far as international tension relaxes.

To commit ourselves to opposing the new capitalism and the new
imperialism here is, at the same time, to make possible a new kind of
discourse with the communist world. Socialists and communists may enter
into common argument, not as opponents and outsiders in each other's
systems, but as friends in a common cause.

A critical conflict is now taking place, not only between states, as in
the tragic division between the Soviet Union and China, but within these
societies. We do not want or expect the Soviet Union to come to resemble

western capitalist societies, though we welcome the increasing prosperity of the Soviet people and the technical advances of its economy - advances which demonstrate that social and economic growth, in the modern world, are wider and more rational processes than in the limited vision of the new capitalism. At the same time, the remaking of Soviet society remains urgent, and in expressing our opposition to its disciplinary and manipulative features we are also expressing support for, and confidence in, the growing volume of democratic criticism within that society.

In moving out of the fixed defensive responses of the past, we are looking for friends and allies, not among states but among peoples. As Isaac Deutscher declared (at the Berkeley Teach-in on Vietnam, in May 1965):

> The division may perhaps once again run *within* nations rather than *between* nations. And once the divisions begin to run within nations, progress begins anew ... progress towards a socialist world, towards *one socialist world.*

In western Europe and the United States this progress will be voiced by all those who act, to the limit of their powers, against the involvement of their own governments in the strategy of imperialism. In Russia and in Eastern Europe the voice may be more muffled - sometimes in devious ways and through opaque censorship - of those who are working to dismantle the obsolete structures and ideology of war dictatorship and of forced industrialization.

Our own allegiance can be given no more to any partial description of international crisis, but only to a total description in which both movements of resistance are seen - and are seen to converge - so that a socialism that is both democratic and revolutionary can be realized as international aspiration and actuality.

In many different ways, then, from the most immediate to the most permanent issues, there are alternative policies, alternative emphases and directions of energy, which it must be our duty to connect. But it is not enough to list policies. We are serious, any of us, to the extent that we are able to build, on the basis of these policies, an increasingly effective and alternative political system - a real opposition - which is capable, in these urgent months and years, of working towards the necessary pressure and breakthrough, in the orthodox political system we oppose. And here, as we shall see, there are quite special difficulties. There are alternative policies, but what are the politics of implementing them?

42. Against managed politics

The whole point, about politics now, is that, in opposition, there is a radical gap between consciousness and organization: partly because of real changes, and partly because the familiar institutions of the Left have been pressed out of shape and recognition by the society we have been describing.

The political aim of the new capitalism, and of the governments which sustain it, is clear. It is to muffle real conflict, to dissolve it into a false political consensus; to build, not a genuine and radical community of life and interest, but a bogus conviviality between every social group. Consensus politics, integral to the success of the new capitalism, is in its essence manipulative politics, the politics of man-management, and as such deeply undemocratic. Governments are still elected, M.P.s assert the supremacy of the House of Commons. But the real business of government is the management of consensus between the most powerful and organized elites.

In a consensual society, the ruling elites can no longer impose their will by coercion: but neither will they see progress as a people organizing itself for effective participation in power and responsibility. Democracy, indeed, becomes a structure to be negotiated and manoeuvred. The task of the leading politicians is to build around each issue by means of bargain and compromise a coalition of interests, and especially to associate the large units of power with their legislative programme.

Consensus politics thus becomes the politics of incremental action: it is not programmed for any large-scale structural change. It is the politics of pragmatism, of the successful manoeuvre within existing limits. Every administrative act is a kind of clever performance, an exercise of political public relations. Whether the manoeuvres are made by a Tory or Labour government then hardly matters, since both accept the constraints of the *status quo* as a framework. Government, as the Prime Minister often reminds us, is simply the determination 'to govern'. The circle of politics has been closed.

It has been closed in a very special way. There have always, in capitalist society, been separate sources of power, based on property and control, with which governments must negotiate. But the whole essence of the new capitalism is an increasing rationalization and co-ordination of just this structure. The states within the state, the high commands in each sector - the banks, the corporations, the federations of industrialists, the T.U.C. - are given a new and more formal place in the political structure, and this, increasingly, is the actual machinery of decision-making: in their own fields, as always, but now also in a co-ordinated field. This political structure, which is to a decisive extent mirrored in the ownership and control of public communications, is then plausibly described as 'the national interest'. And it is not only that the national interest has then been defined so as to include the very specific and often damaging interests of the banks, the combines, the City; but also so as to *exclude* what, on the other side, are called 'sectional' or 'local' interests: of the poor, of particular workers, of backward regions. The elected element - the democratic process which is still offered as ratifying - gets redefined, after its passage through the machines, as one interest among others: what is still, in an abstract way, called the public interest, but present now only as one - relatively weak and ill-organized - among several elements involved in effective decisions.

In this process, the policies of the two major parties, but also the parties themselves and their auxiliary institutions, are in an advanced stage of adjustment to the demands of managed capitalism. Free-market capitalism could tolerate, in the nineteenth century, a free market also in political ideas and policies. Within this framework, adjustments of interest could be made without excessive tension; and what the forms allowed, the long democratic pressures of the British people endowed with greater content. Within these forms, but only after repeated failures, and the most determined struggles, the Labour party finally emerged as a party of working-class interests.

But capitalism in our own time has repented of its youth. The old kind of political conflict introduces uncertainty into planning and continually reactivates centres of resistance to its dispositions. Just as new capitalism finds it increasingly necessary to forecast and at times to create demand, so in its political expression it finds it necessary not to adjust to but to create what it calls public opinion. And in doing this, unprecedented means of persuasion lie to hand.

The first outlines of new capitalism became visible, to many of us, through what was happening in communications. In the struggle for democracy in the nineteenth century, dissenting minorities and the new popular organizations had, if not equality, at least some comparative opportunity of access to the places where opinion was formed: the cheap printing press, the hustings, the soapbox, the chapel, the public hall. Many of these means are of course still open, but the main channels of fact and persuasion are now very different, in television, the national press, the monolithic political party. Opposition groups may get an occasional hearing, in any one of these, but normally on the terms of the established system. On Vietnam, for example, we have had to buy advertising space in the newspapers. On television, the occasional dissenter will be interviewed, but as part of the passing show, which is normally following the existing contours of opinion. Balance, as a principle of public service broadcasting, is balance between representatives of the parties, or at most sections of the parties. All the widely distributed newspapers are in capitalist hands, and conduct their own continual campaigns and pressures.

To be outside this system, and against its values, may allow, at times, a brief invitation to join in, or to have dissenting views processed by the established commentators. More commonly, it allows what is said to be ignored, in the confidence that the small-circulation pamphlet, the serious book, the meeting in a hired hall, will not get through to the majority of people, in ways that would make the suppression obvious. And when, because of this, we go out into the streets, a hundred thousand people, to campaign against nuclear weapons, we are reported and placed as an eccentric group, a traditional rite of Easter, an event in the Labour party.

For that is the point, in the mode of opinion-formation under new capitalism. The system is offered as absolute; it, and only it, is normality. In open and free debate, such normality might be challenged, but this precise new capitalism - a working partnership of public and private bureaucracy, in defence of established political and economic interests - has the major communications system safely in its own hands, at a level of organization and cost which makes any challenge to it, from the beginning, unofficial, marginal, even petty. It seems a kind of arrogance, in such a climate, to stand up on one's own terms, and offer an opinion at the level of any other.

'Who are these people anyway?': the conditioned response has been learned. In fact the answer is simple: people like any others, all needing to be heard. Yet to state the principle now is the most absolute challenge; every device of habit, pretended amusement, false political realism, interest in a job, will be deployed against it. Anything not in the system is unofficial, amateur, voluntary or extremist, and so can be written down and out. With a proper instinct for where they really belong, the regular commentators, the men 'inside' politics, return public attention to such crucial matters as who is now Number Three or Number Four in the Cabinet; who, lately, has talked himself into or out of a job; how the interests, next Tuesday and especially next Friday, are going to be balanced up; and, at moderate intervals, will the election be autumn or spring? It is in that drugged atmosphere that the struggle for new policies, for an effective democratic campaign, has now to be undertaken.

43. Voters, representatives and others

'But democracy means parliament.' Isn't that the usual answer? At a formal level it appears that democratic parliamentary politics continue. Of course, in a special way, which has always been meant to limit popular power. When there has been an election, and a new government comes in, it is taken for granted that some of its leading members will be people who have not been elected at all: Lords Boodle and Doodle, as Dickens once called them; or Lords Home and Snow, Chalfont and Salisbury, who have arrived by another route altogether. A second Chamber, as it is still called, is there already, irrespective of the election: the Lords born to rule, or at least to have the right of entry to where legislation is confirmed. There is now some change in this: instead of all the hereditary peers (though many of these will remain) there will be life peers and even - breath-catching in its modernity - life peeresses. And this, it is said, is a democratic advance. It shows how far we have gone. For in fact, of course, it is simply the organized development of political patronage. Mr X, from here or there - a defeated candidate, a retired official, a friend of a friend, a member of many committees - is transformed into the name of a river, a town or a mountain, but transformed for a purpose. The party leaders hand out, and are known to hand out, titles and political jobs, in one operation. They hand them out in a sector - a qualifying sector - of the supposedly open democratic process.

Meanwhile, in Lords and Commons alike, the process goes on in an atmosphere heavy with rituals, and these are more than picturesque survivals; they are meant to lower the voice, to bow the knee, to stilt the language of reality; to confirm a closed circle, as against the pressures of a noisy popular world. This is the theatrical show in which a precise power is mediated; the mellow dusk in which actual power is blurred. Many people in Britain now see it for what it is. The young, especially, see and criticize it; they are less deferential, and these particular rituals - from Black Rod to the Queen's Speech, and from the Right Honourable Gentleman to the Victorian stained glass - have little surviving respect.

But we are then asked to believe, by men within the system, that our criticism of parliament is some sort of 'dangerous sign': the symptom of a growing disbelief in democracy, or of cynicism and apathy. On the contrary, the criticism of parliament is in the interest of democracy as something other than a ritual. It is not just the style but the effect of the institutions that we are really opposing. For in its very rituals, parliament now reveals its claim - its inadmissible claim - to consume all other political activity and organization for the convenience of its own procedures. What it claimed in the past, to get rid of Old Corruption, it now rationalizes to limit any further development of democracy. What enabled it to operate, in a laissez-faire society, is now the means of its decline, in a more tightly organized capitalist world.

Thus we would very willingly admit the power and the importance of the House of Commons if it would show some signs of political action in general terms, as opposed to what it takes to be significant within its own terms. We can conceive, and would like to see, a House of Commons embattled against organized private power or established interests; fighting a popular cause against arbitrary authority and secret decision. But it is not only that we never see this, in any central or critical case (it survives in some marginal cases, and these show what might be done). It is that we are asked to take seriously, as members like others in the whole body of 'representatives', men who were elected on one programme and now keep their place on another; who in practice submit their convictions to a five-year electoral cycle; who speak against a policy and then fail to vote against it, or even sometimes vote for it; who, even in passionate opposition, are unable to make the break from rituals and procedures which are there to tame them. We are told we have parliamentary government, but all we can say is that we would like to see some. As it is now operating, parliament is acquiescing, openly, in the disappearance of effective parliamentary government, and in its replacement by managed politics.

Representative democracy, as it is now interpreted, seems to us very clearly the surviving sign and medium of a class society. The representative part is got over as quickly as possible, and at long intervals. It is based on an electoral system which in fact gives very unequal representation, and which effectively fails to represent any sufficiently scattered minority. It is in any case at once qualified by co-option and inheritance from elsewhere. What then takes over, as normality, is a closed style. And this is where representative democracy, in its very decline and in its acceptance of decline, can be comfortably absorbed by the new managed politics. It claims too little, and then finds it has lost even that. In separating itself from continuing popular pressure, it becomes emptied of the urgent and substantial popular content which would enable it to resist or control the administrative machine. It does not really participate in government; it mainly receives and reacts to decisions from elsewhere. And this, though tragic, is a kind of justice, for it has prepared its own impotence, by substituting its representative rituals for the reality of participating democracy anywhere. The mood which now questions parliament, and which can eventually transform and save it, is indeed this new democratic emphasis: on participation in decisions, wherever they are being made, by those who are going to be involved in the results. This needs a new creation and flexibility of institutions, to make democratic practice effective throughout the society, by activity and by locality, rather than in some closed, centralized, ritualized place. If the House of Commons were the ultimate focus of this democratic practice, on the great national issues, it would quite quickly regain its importance. But while it prefers to remain with a different system and to accept its quite different rules and styles, it will go on emptying itself of democratic reality.

For the irony is that these ritualized representative institutions are now being steadily converted to machines which even within themselves give the illusion but never the fact of democratic participation. What ordinary people want and elect (from a choice already processed by this style of politics) is seen as a factor, but only a factor, in what is going to happen; one element in a conflict of interests. This conflict is not between desire and reality. It is between some people's wills and others: between an elected programme and what the bankers want, what industry wants, what the 'experts' want, what the civil servants want, and what the Americans want. The government is then not the people in power, but a broker, a co-ordinator, a part of the machine. What can then be achieved - the process is of course not complete - is the final expropriation of the people's active political presence. Instead, we shall have a new technocratic politics, fitted into the modern state. It is a politics which would replace, even at the formal level, all older theories of the sovereignty of the people through their elected representatives. It offers, instead, a congress of representatives of the new capitalist state and its consequent political relations. These will, of course, often quarrel among themselves, and the rest of us may be asked to take sides. But all actual choice will be directed towards the resolution of conflicts within that specific machinery.

We then confront a whole system which is foreclosing upon democracy, and which is expropriating the people of their political identity. We do not mean to signal the danger of a rebirth of fascism, the armed authoritarianism of the thirties. The authoritarianism of the sixties is altogether more bland. It does not come with knuckle-dusters and revolvers but with political sedatives and processing. It does not segregate dissenters in concentration camps, but allows them to segregate themselves in little magazines and sectarian societies. It does not require of its supporters that they should march through the streets, but simply that they should be apathetic. Government? Our governors will do that for us.

44. Two meanings of social democracy

This managed political system, which we are now experiencing, forces us to look again at the meaning of social democracy. The contrast we have inherited, in the socialist movement, is between social democracy and communism; but we have now to insist on another contrast, between two kinds of social democracy.

It has always been argued that the critical choice, for a socialist, is between a programme of violent change - the capture of state power - and a programme of electoral change - the winning of a majority in parliament. Tactics, values, organization seem to hang on that choice; the shape of a future society is prefigured by the road we choose.

In effect, however, this choice is never made in the abstract. The alternatives only open, in any realistic way, in societies which have open electoral processes and the necessary freedoms of speech and association. And even then it is not a question of two polar kinds of society: the free and the authoritarian. In political reality, there is a complicated range from societies in which no legal and open struggle is possible, through societies in which there are local and marginal opportunities for democratic organization, to societies, like our own, in which the opportunities are in one sense completely open but in practice are modified by concentrations of capital and by effective reserve and emergency powers.

No single socialist strategy can be realistically asserted, against so wide a range of reality. There are many places in the world where an underground organization or an armed struggle is inevitable. Western socialists have acknowledged this fact only with difficulty or reluctance. The necessary methods, in such a situation, are so foreign to their own immediate experience that they often spend more time deploring the methods than attacking the society from which they flow. The most immediate occasion, for this crisis of choice, is in southern Africa, where, for historical reasons, British socialists are directly involved and where it is British government policy that has left a majority movement to struggle on its own and as it can.

But the full dimension of this choice is as wide as the twentieth century. Social democracy was, after all, historically the parent of communism. The forms of struggle and order which we now associate with communism - with the choice of an armed revolutionary strategy - were responses, above all, to brutal authoritarian and military régimes. In the process, undoubtedly, a dimension of socialism was lost. The forms of socialist order which came out of this historical experience required a continuing and difficult socialist critique, and at times opposition. We had to express our solidarity with comrades who were struggling to overcome hardened, obsolete and persistently arbitrary forms of the new power. We could hold no brief to defend an armed bureaucracy, or a police state, in the name of socialism. Yet, precisely because we were in a historical position to do this, we could fail to notice our own historical determinants. What we had to say, against arbitrary power, could be a means to the development of the socialism itself, but only if we defined our situation by something more than a negative; only if we could show, in practice, that alternative socialist forms were available, were uncompromising, and had serious chances of success. Nobody can underestimate the difficulties, on either side; but it has to be said, of western social democratic movements, that they have been better at the negative than at the positive demonstration. The easy product of the historical situation - the emphasis on personal freedom and open democracy - has been widely apparent, while the hard product - the maintenance of a serious socialism, in and through these values - has been much more difficult to find.

And then it is at just this point that the two meanings of social democracy most clearly reveal themselves. For social democracy can be that form of socialist struggle which is available as a serious option in societies which have relatively open democratic institutions and the necessary freedoms to use them. Or it can be the gradual assimilation of socialism to the forms of the society which it began by opposing: an assimilation sustained, not by historical analysis where we are, but by an abstract contrast with the forms of revolutionary socialism in very different situations. What this latter kind of social democracy most insists on is its difference from revolutionary socialism: not as a historical difference, but as an abstract political choice. What it draws attention to in itself are the features which it shares with a liberal or capitalist democracy; what it modifies, in this act of association, are the commitments and content of its socialism. The necessary emphasis on democratic rights and institutions is made to cover the effective abandonment of any socialist intentions. Slowly, a social democratic party can reach the point where associations to the right seem natural; associations to the left impossible. As in Britain, it can seem much more shocking, to a good Labour man, to be found talking or working with a Communist than with a Tory; and this, at least, is no longer an abstract preference; it has the regularity of practice.

In societies like our own, with parliamentary and other openly elected institutions, and with effective freedoms of democratic organization and publication, the choice for socialists is not the abstract choice, of so much received theory. It is only at the level of unthinking repetition that the choice between 'revolution', in its traditional sense of a violent capture of state power, and 'evolution', in its traditional sense of the inevitability of gradual change towards socialist forms, can survive. These are not, and have not for some time been, available socialist strategies, in societies of this kind. Western Communist parties, defining the road to socialism as they see it, no longer think of the violent capture of state power. But this change has been more widely noticed than the other. Western social democratic parties no longer think of an inevitable, gradual change towards socialist forms; on the contrary, they offer themselves as governing parties within the existing social system, which they will at once improve and modify, but in no serious sense replace.

The two meanings of social democracy then stare us in the face. Under the cover of a traditional and repetitive contrast between 'violent' and 'parliamentary' means, the necessary argument about a socialist strategy has been severely displaced. There are acrimonious disputes about other situations and other times, but the positive meaning of a democratic socialism is overridden by two negatives: the contrast with communism, and the emptying assimilation to capitalism. It is clear that we can no longer afford this kind of displacement. We have to begin the definition again, in our own historical situation.

And here the first fact that is apparent is that the 'parliamentary' strategy, in its ordinary forms, has been overtaken and nullified by the internal development of managed capitalism. It made sense to talk of winning power through a parliamentary majority when it was possible to believe that it was in parliament that effective power really lay. But, as we have seen, the apparently open democratic process of parliament is being steadily replaced, in practice but also in theory, by a new and interlocking set of governing institutions: what we have called the congress of a modern capitalist state and its political nominees. Control of parliament is certainly necessary, if this congress is to function. It is ironic to remember that Labour's political and economic policies were much less openly declared and executed in the parliament elected in 1964, when it had only a tiny majority, than in the parliament elected in 1966, when it had what was quite openly called a five-year security to govern. The change of political emphasis, especially in policies towards the trade unions, after the apparently greater democratic victory of 1966, was an unmistakable sign of the new character of contemporary government.

For it is precisely in the assimilation and control of all popular and representative institutions, so that they are not able effectively to disturb the process of corporate government, that the politics of the new capitalism resides. The political parties, and parliament itself, are necessary to legitimate this essentially centralized and bureaucratic form of government, and the problem is how to get through this process of legitimacy to the point where ministers, civil servants, public authority executives, and the centralized organs of industry and the unions can negotiate and govern in their own terms. Thus the Labour party was much more responsive to what was called its base in the country when this legitimization was precarious than when, by the very efforts of that base, a long run of legitimacy was assured.

It is then of course obvious that socialists can no longer go on restricting their view of socialist advance to the achievement of more powerful Labour majorities in parliament. The drive for what is called strong government, and political stability, is in this continuing situation reactionary; for what is meant by these terms, in the institutions we now have, is an insulation from *popular* pressures, so that the consensus with *established* interests can be effectively carried through.

The consequences for social democracy are then very serious. With no other political strategy but the winning of a parliamentary majority, it is, as a movement, with its habitual forms of activity geared solely to the electoral process, acquiescing in the precise mechanisms which are intended to contain it.

The central contradiction of the politics of the new capitalism is its need for electoral legitimacy. In its internal mechanisms, it is already in a position to surpass what has been understood by democracy altogether, and to replace it by methods which it uses in its economic activities: market research, the taking of consumer opinion; in political terms, an effectively permanent governing bureaucracy, which takes account of public opinion not in active ways, by offering direct choices, but in planned ways, by polling opinion. The opinion poll is different from an election because it leads, and can lead, to no open change; at the same time it allows the governing bureaucracy to know its room for manoeuvre, and to estimate what is necessary in building a public opinion which is organized only in relation to itself, and which has no obvious means of acting in directly effective ways. Technically, this is all a new capitalist government now needs; its ideologists and commentators already speak with impatience of the disturbance caused by elections and open political conflict. But, politically, the legitimization of government, by democratic processes, is still inevitable; and it is here that the crisis of social democracy is now right in the open.

It is not simply a question of programmes and ideologies: these can be argued about, endlessly, in the party press and at party conferences, for they no longer go to the heart of the matter; the elected government has been given the right to govern in its own terms. It is primarily a question of institutions, for what is needed by the system is an intermittently available and in that sense efficient electoral machine, which by traditional inertia is still called a party but which must by no means become a serious political party in the sense of posing an alternative organization and campaign. If the party becomes real, as a campaigning democratic institution, it is at once a focus of genuinely alternative power. On the other hand, if it is to be a still mainly voluntary electoral machine, to what extent can it be emptied of a real political programme, which its members take seriously and expect, after their work, to be carried through?

Behind the traditional discussion of social democracy, and of its differences from communism, a far more urgent and serious decision is in effect now being taken. It is not in the obsolete perspective of the choice between 'revolution' and 'evolution', but in the actual perspective of the choice between a political movement and an electoral machine, that we have to look, in Britain, at the situation and condition of the Labour party.

45. The Labour Party

New capitalism and managed politics, in their present forms, could never have been established if Labour had remained a party within which democratic processes moved with freedom and fluency: a party capable of articulating the aspirations and grievances of the working people. We do not mean that the pressures of new capitalism would have been any less strong, but that the critical decision - to adapt to or resist them - would have opened along the line between the two major parties. A serious political movement would then have corresponded to traditional electoral needs; the electoral struggle, in all important respects, would have been at the centre of the political struggle as a whole. But the reverse has happened: the official Labour party, though by no means its whole membership, has redefined itself to fit in with new capitalism and managed politics. The party created, as it was thought, to transform society, and still the party of the great majority - some 60 to 70 per cent - of the working people of Britain, faces us now in this alien form: a voting machine; an effective bureaucracy; an administration claiming no more than to run the existing system more efficiently.

The difficulties of socialists have seemed to flow from this paradox: that the major working-class party, in which many socialists still work, has been absorbed, at the level of government and political decision, into the structures of capitalist politics.

The development of the current Labour government - it is perhaps better to call it, in traditional terms, an administration - has confirmed this fact of absorption, but this is no sudden evolution. It has been clear for a long time that the Labour party is a compromise between working-class objectives and the traditional power structure: the first, it has often been hoped, could be achieved through the second. It has been possible in the past to see this as a necessary tension: the only way change can come. But what is more and more evident is that, in effective politics, this tension has gone.

The idea of socialism has not been abandoned - that was the straightforward gesture of adaptation (the excision of Clause Four) which was tried, and failed, under Gaitskell. With Wilson, socialism has been quietly written out, allowed to lapse. And it is now given out - not so much in argument as in mood - that socialism is in any case an outdated conception, outside any realistic political structure. Or, where an appearance of continuity seems necessary, to keep the party together, a kind of upside-down definition is adopted: whatever the Labour Government now does is socialism: do not the Conservatives and the right-wing newspapers still call them socialists?

No coherent analysis of capitalist power, no movement of socialist education and propaganda, no authentic ideology of social change, has emerged from the institutional Labour party for two decades. Whatever has emerged (like the New Left) has been the initiative of individuals working outside the party's institutional framework, who have improvised their own organizations, and who have been regarded by the officialdom of Labour with distrust or (as in the case of several initiatives among the young socialists) with actual proscription. Everything, in fact, has been subordinated to a single purpose: the building and management of a popular electoral machine.

It has been obvious, of course, since the late forties: how like each other, in this central respect, the Labour and Tory parties have become. To tune in on their arguments is to find discord of a kind: endless battles of percentages, as between the first eighteen months of Labour and the last eighteen months of Tory; as between the scandalous mismanagement and the wise and steady efficiency of whoever at that moment are government and opposition, and vice versa - let the speeches be replayed. Each of course wants to win, and on the lines between them there are some real issues, which should not be underestimated; a change of government brings some important differences of emphasis, and a few actual changes of policy. But from outside their system, it is increasingly apparent that each, in major respects, continues the central policies of the other: only of course those are not policies, subject to political challenge; they are 'the realities of the situation', which cannot be touched by 'the art of the possible'. What we then have are two parties who basically agree about the structure and purposes of society, but who disagree about many secondary policies, about details of administration, and, crucially, about each other's capacities. An older political language, of ideas and of principles, is derided as 'theology'. The new language is technical: of mutual competence and incompetence; of dynamism and purposiveness, of drift and muddle. Of course, when two parties want to do much the same things, they are likely to argue even more sharply at this level; on the relative skills of the two sets of bosses.

The extraordinary thing then is that thousands of people still turn out at nights or week-ends, and work to exhaustion during actual campaigns, to appear to join in that kind of conflict. In fact, while some of this is habitual loyalty, and some again an expectation of patronage, most of it is still an attempt, by politically interested people, to endow the dead forms with some real content. Moreover, at elections, as on Sundays and at conferences, the older language tends miraculously to reappear. For a time, even, the choices do appear historic. There is then all the more bitterness, as in these last years, when the system reasserts itself and leaves its electioneering behind. And in the Labour party especially: for whereas a party whose members have substantial interests in the existing system can afford to be, need be no other than, an electoral machine, a party which has been built on aspiration and on ideas of a different future will in such a case, in its existing forms, die.

It is only necessary to imagine, in a utopian sense, what a democratic mass party of socialist and working-class aspiration - capable of confronting managed capitalism - would be like, to disclose, by contrast, the present predicament. Such a party would draw strength from active, committed groups not only in the communities but also in places of work. Such groups (quite as much as the national organs of the party) would engage in the continuous work of education and agitation necessary to disclose the incompatibility between human and capitalist priorities. A first call upon the resources (both intellectual and organizational) of such a party would be the establishment of a national daily newspaper capable of organizing demand and of disseminating through the society alternative, socialist descriptions of reality. The reason why the dissolution of the *Daily Herald* caused so little anxiety, even in the Labour movement, is that it had long ceased to do that, or anything like that. So far from suspicion or repression, such a party would welcome - could not, indeed, function without - the self-activating initiatives of socialist shop stewards, intellectuals, and student and youth movements. Above all, such a party would seek in all its activities to enlist the active democratic participation - in nationalized industries, in university and educational structures, in municipal and community affairs - of the people in their own self-government. And what it sought to extend, in democratic actualities, throughout the society would be expressed also in its own internal structure. Its leadership would be clearly accountable to the party's effective and active membership, drawing upon their experience and controlled by their criticism.

As a model this may be utopian: but there is no longer any point in pretending that there is any correspondence, of the most distant kind, between the model and the actuality of the Labour party. Over the years, the commitment of members has been dissipated: in part, by the bureaucratic character of the machine; in part, by actual political disillusion and victimization; most generally, by the apathy provoked by a party which has no use for the intelligence of its own members, but only - and then only in election times - for their dutiful feet. Since the early 1950s, there has been a very marked decline in individual party membership. At the same time, in step with the new managed politics, the party machine can afford to rely less and less upon individual members, and even upon its constituency structures. As the new-style campaigning comes to rely less on personal activity, and more on effective use of television, publicity and the press, the machine grows in importance at the expense of the base. This is reflected, as throughout managed politics, in the character of the party. Just as power no longer resides in parliament, but the elected element is only one factor among other interest groups, so a parallel process has been reproduced and re-emphasized within the structure of the Labour party. Power is not in its Conference - the party equivalent of parliament - but in its executive leadership. The business of Conference (as the political commentators make clear) is not to decide policy but to project the public image. The interesting questions are how party leaders will manage their critics, and how they will neutralize any resolution passed against the platform. In this they can count (as Gaitskell could on unilateral disarmament) upon the unabashed support of the media, in the name of the 'national interest' and consensus politics. The parliamentary party can disregard Conference decisions, since parliament is, supposedly, responsible not to a party but to an electorate. The party leadership can disregard advice from its national executive or the parliamentary party, since it is in possession of secret information and it is its business to 'govern'. But the individual member of parliament who seeks to vote against the government (on an issue of political principle, and one which, perhaps, accords with his own pledges to the electorate) can be immediately threatened with deprivation of party rights. In any such case, a constituency party must be quick to support its member, and to combine with others in the defence and formulation of socialist policies. But the regular denial of democratic principles is not the result of accident; it is intrinsic to a machinery designed for just these purposes. As Richard Crossman has written:

> The Labour Party required militants - politically conscious socialists to do the work of organizing the constituencies. But since these militants tended to be 'extremists', a constitution was needed which maintained their enthusiasm by apparently creating a full party democracy while excluding them from effective power.

Here, even cynically, the rationality - and not just the accident - of the existing machinery is described. The description could be profitably hung in every committee room; but for what purpose?

To show party workers what they are up against, and how they need to recover control of the movement they still maintain? But if that were the conclusion, they would need also to be shown how. For it is not as if a great democratic party has failed to kick against its incorporation. Repeated battles have been fought in and out of Conference, to remake a democratic party. The historic means of ensuring that Labour should remain a working-class party - the special position of the trade unions in the constitution, and their consequent block votes - has, in a bitter irony, been one of the regular devices for ensuring the defeat of democratic reforms. In the present tension between the party and the unions, this might indeed change, though the grip of habit is strong. But what else might be concluded, in that committee room, staring at that particular text? That one should get up and go? The problem, always, has been where. That one should stay, in a new sober realism: that is how politics are: devilish clever, our leaders, against those clever devils the Tories? This last response, unfortunately, is not caricature. Nor is it always the simple gaping it sounds. It is sometimes the resigned, deferential habit of corporatism: our class against their class, our party against their party; any means - even, in some men, abandonment of policies; abandonment, even, of the tie of party to class - can quite properly be used; only the young and inexperienced think otherwise. And then, related to this, though it is not often mentioned: the flow of patronage, to any party that periodically becomes a government: not only the local government ticket, to all that civic dignity affords; not only the nomination to the magistracy, to the school governors, to the hospital board; but also the connexion, when the leaders need you, to the high places, to the men in power.

Socialists should not, that is to say, have any illusions about the effect of incorporation on the Labour party. Since it has become successful, it contains many different kinds of people. Many socialists are still there, by upbringing or by conviction, seeing no real alternative. But others are also there, as they are there in the government: men who do not mind that it is an electoral machine, whatever for the time being the policies may be, so long as the machine is successful. It is an interesting exercise to measure the degree of disillusion with the government when it publishes a reactionary policy, and when it loses a bye-election. It is possible, of course, to be concerned about both, but it is worth watching and asking.

The fact is, somebody usually says, the Labour party is a coalition. We could wish that were true. Historically, of course, it has seemed to be true. Labour has always contained a range of men and policies from liberal reformers to committed socialists. But this is another effect of incorporation: that what starts as a coalition ends as a confidence trick.

Take those Labour M.P.s who are socialists; take the socialist resolutions passed at party conferences and written into election programmes. If these were, indeed, one element in a coalition, what would follow would be bargaining, negotiation: so much of this policy against so much of that; otherwise, no coalition. But anybody in the Labour party, or in the parliamentary Labour party, knows that this is not how things happen. On the contrary, a consensus is built, around the policies of the leadership. At some critical points, as the consensus forms, the influence of the Left can be felt; assurances, at least, have to be given. But a consensus of that kind, with a bureaucratic machine behind the leadership, is very much easier to run than any real coalition. The final power, in negotiation, would be of withdrawing from the coalition, and thus affecting its strength. But when the machine, effectively, is the whole party, there is nowhere to go but out of the party, even if the policy you stick on is that approved by the majority in a constituency or at conference. Within the system, that kind of threat, which in a real coalition would be effective, can seem a kind of suicide; indeed it is much more often offered as an option by opponents than by friends.

Yet that cannot be the end of the matter. Socialists in the Labour party have been afraid, far too long, of describing it as it is. There has been a continual breeding of illusions and false hopes. In so intractable a problem, with so much at stake, there is of course no easy answer. But the only possibility of an answer comes from telling the truth: describing the incorporation, in terms of policy and of procedures; refusing those spurts of temporary confidence which would show it other than it is; and then, in that mood, following the argument through, taking the necessary action, wherever it leads.

46. Other radical groupings

Given the assimilation of the Labour party to the orthodox structures of British society, two developments were inevitable: the formation of other radical groupings and the formation of other socialist groupings. We can look at the radical groupings first.

At a national level the most persistent offering of a radical position has been that of the Liberal party. Just because by its electoral weakness it was disengaged from some of the orthodox structures, it was able to take up certain radical issues which often put it in practice to the left of the Labour party. In the last year or so the Young Liberals have pushed this even further and have come to represent a clear and important body of radical opinion. But two qualifications have then to be made. First, that in this very development, relations between a campaigning radical movement and an orthodox parliamentary leadership became critical. Second, that in this crisis the vagueness of the radical commitment became obvious. There was, for example, a critical clash on so fundamental a point as whether the Liberal party supported capitalism.

In its effective direction the Liberal Party was quite clearly capitalist. Most of its characteristic policies - support of the Common Market, 'partnership in industry' and trade union reform - were indeed of a specifically new capitalist kind. Yet in other matters, such as democratic regional government and opposition to bureaucracy, it was developing responses which were bound to question any capitalist state. In its critique of foreign policy it was in practice questioning some aspects of the imperialist alliance. The miscellaneity of its whole policy was then very apparent. The consequent crisis within the party is then largely repeating similar crises within Left and radical opinion as a whole.

A more significant response has been the development of nationalist parties in Scotland and Wales. It is clear that the young people, especially, who are going into these parties take with them the radicalism which finds no adequate expression elsewhere. Moreover, their expectations are reasonable, in that Scotland and Wales have been politically and economically deprived by the existing system, so that within these countries a national appeal is inevitably a radical appeal. Nothing is more stupid than the stock response of some London-based Labour party people that nationalism of this kind is in some way ominous or that such descriptions as 'incipient fascism' can be used to characterize it. In real policies, what the nationalist parties are demanding is a necessary and inevitable challenge to a centralized managed politics and to a capitalism which, creating prosperity in favoured regions, creates poverty in unfavoured. The Scottish and Welsh nationalists are fortunate in being able to bring to these general protests that sense of a national identity which can quickly cross and dissolve existing political affiliations. At the same time they are of course in danger of the wrong kind of emphasis on what 'national' feeling is. Like all parties based on the sentiments of an exploited and identifiable group, they will eventually face crises of direction, in internal policy, of the kind already familiar elsewhere. There will be Scots and Welsh to oppose, as well as 'the English'; and there will be English to ally with. Yet for some years ahead, based firmly on the correspondence of their national aspirations with a well-grounded general opposition to the priorities of present British society, their political success and their growing support can be wholeheartedly welcomed.

From radical parties we move to radical campaigns. These have been a striking feature of the last decade, and reveal more clearly than anything else the failure of the existing political system to represent the political needs of a mature democratic society. Characteristically most of these campaigns have centred on a single issue: world hunger, colonial freedom, racial equality, nuclear disarmament, child poverty, homelessness. Between them they have created a political consciousness which has made the programmes of the parties seem tired and limited. Yet there are obvious difficulties in the relation between these campaigns and the orthodox political structures. We can see these more clearly if we distinguish between types of single-issue campaign.

The first type is the establishment of a liberal or radical national presence. Characteristically it collects the signatures of prominent persons, holds national meetings and press conferences, and lobbies parliament directly or indirectly. Its whole style assumes a permeable political system on which 'influential' opinion can be brought effectively to bear. A second type extends its presence to local organization and branch activity, thus moving beyond the style appropriate to membership of a ruling or 'influential' class. Working now directly on public opinion, it still assumes in the end a permeable system; it is campaigning for the adjustment of this or that priority within a general politics which still commands support. A third type, often beginning in these ways, develops into a campaign which questions the whole politics of the system, in the light of its chosen issue. The most evident example of this third type is the Campaign for Nuclear Disarmament, which, however, always retained elements of the two other types.

Paradoxically, the test of any single-issue campaign, in the existing political system, is the point at which it appears to fail. It will have done, in any case, certain important work: in extending consciousness, or in making some actual changes. But in none of the issues on which the important campaigns have been organized is complete success possible without a radical challenge to the *system* of priorities of the society. As this point is reached, it is natural that each of the campaigns should undergo a crucial development. It can remain as a focus of conscientious dissent, with the danger of being used as a safety valve. Or, pushing its issue right through, it reaches the point where it contradicts its own definition and is no longer a single-issue but a general campaign.

At the same time, campaigns of the second and third types have been invaluable centres of local democratic organization in a period in which the politics of the parties has been steadily evolving towards a centralized bureaucratic machinery. As such, the campaigns are in structure as much as in issues more alive than the ruling political system, and can be seen as to some extent mobilizing the experience if not yet the will to challenge it. They take their place in this respect with the many organizations working inside ordinary society, which are also a response to an increasingly formal or incomplete democracy. The new organizations of many kinds of professional workers and of students; the vitally important community and neighbourhood projects; the associations of parents, tenants and residents; the research groups and societies which organize national intellectual networks: all these in their different ways are claims on the substance of a democratic politics which must be seen as vital points of growth. This work from local and special-interest centres, outwards, often intersects the older campaigns working from a national presence, again outwards but along a different conception of society. The local groups and special-interest centres and projects are not 'new constituencies', though they have sometimes been called so; they do not exist to put somebody else in power, but to extend, from real centres, their own demands. The point of crisis usually comes in the way these demands are followed up. The willingness to demonstrate, for example, in active, uncompromising and hostile ways, is usually central to any real growth.

Demonstration has its own difficulties. The demonstrations of C.N.D. and the Committee of 100 were a new and effective political style, but there is always the danger of demonstration declining to a mere style, and so being insulated. Demonstration is important when it involves real confrontation; in a place where some power exists, and when an active presence is assembled against it. The demonstrations on Vietnam, at the Greek Embassy, and at the air bases, in which the Committee of 100 and others have been active, were of this character, and were viciously opposed by the State, in imprisonment and other ways. We stand with this kind of radical political action, and will seek to extend it.

On the other hand, what can also happen is a self-enclosed demonstration of difference or dissent, which, though it may be locally valuable, can be quickly absorbed, as an occasional or marginal routine. This connects with the important fact that a display of external and marginal difference from orthodox society is now so widespread among certain groups: a demonstration of drop-out from the society rather than of active opposition. We believe that important areas of radical experience will go on being locked in this limited demonstration, unless the problems of a more general and active radicalism can be effectively solved.

For the proliferation of radical groupings and 'radical' attitudes is not primarily a matter of organization; it is a matter of experience. It is not just the inadequacy of the Labour party, but the deeper inadequacy of political consciousness in a sharply transitional society, which has thrown up these symptoms. Because the central character of the transition is not seen, there is a continual fragmentation and deflection of social experience, which reappears in the forms of personal or 'special-interest' definitions. Just as the general human claims of displaced or redundant workers seem to be no more than locally defensive (and are then derided as 'backward-looking' by the apologists of the system), so the social contradictions between the skills of research workers, technicians and planners and the difficulties they encounter in real decision-making seem to be no more than the demands of a new elite (and can be rationalized and played on as if the demands of new capitalism, of 'the American future', were their informed demands). These two kinds of radical feeling could hardly be further apart, in style, but they run back to the same root, as do the related experiences and difficulties of professional social workers and teachers, who again know priorities from their daily experience, and in the general difficulty of connecting these with actual decision-making can react as if they were arguing for their own status and importance (and so be played off against others) when what they really represent, in experience and demand, is a necessary phase of social growth.

The situation of students is now very similar. More perhaps than any other group, they have rejected, actively or passively, the proffered goals and self-definitions of the society; they have in many cases withdrawn from them as contemptible or absurd, and present either a loose general scepticism or a more active demand for what is called student power. Once again they are reacted to, as in the case of each other group and even between such groups, as if they were seeking only a special interest, and a privileged one. They are told that they are being charitably supported and should be grateful, and are then often guilty, as other disturbed groups are guilty. Yet students represent at least two critical processes in the society: as the articulate group which in its potential understanding - its role as a new generation with access to the critical human perspectives which higher education ought especially to provide - is inevitably the point of growth of a society understanding and valuing itself; and as a sharply selected group, concentrating all the built-in class factors of current education, which is not prepared to write off its own work or intelligence, but which equally is not prepared to put these at the humble service of ends and institutions controlled by quite different criteria. That resentment against a class system of education should be directed against students rather than against those who actually determine and operate it is confusing enough. That their active and necessary criticism of the society should, like the comparable withdrawals and scepticism of many others of their generation, be displaced to platitudes about the 'don't care' young is even more damaging. As in all these cases of diffused radicalism, the caring is great, and it is where there is a lack of connexion between this serious experience and the possibilities of meaningful action that there are negative and merely affronting (as opposed to confronting) demonstrations.

The case of racial consciousness is again similar. Historically there have been centuries of oppression of the native peoples of Asia, America and Africa, and of those who were dragged from their homes into a distant slavery. Against this, necessarily, there is now active revolt, and against all the distortions, prejudices, discriminations which have followed from it. To be with that revolt against oppression, prejudice and discrimination, in any form and anywhere, is now imperative. But this is only one aspect of 'race', as it now comes through to us. In Britain, the immigrant poor are living out, more sharply than any other identifiable group, the whole range of a general social deprivation: in the decaying centres of cities, in overcrowded schools, in bad housing, in the low wages of unskilled work. Yet this experience, which is in fact a concentration of a general problem of the society, and which is imposed, in similar ways, on other groups of the unsettled poor, is displaced, internally and externally, by the false consciousness of skin colour. That the division between rich and poor in the world is between some of the 'white race' and a majority of all colours, but mainly black, yellow and brown, feeds into this consciousness: as a fact, certainly, but as a fact which can be displaced to its least critical, though not least explosive, element. Not the poverty of the Asian, American and African lands, and the political and economic system which causes it, but its shadow, the 'colour question', is then emphasized and isolated. Not the social experience of the most recently arrived and most exposed members of our own society, but the fact that they are 'coloured' immigrants, is seized on to confuse and deflect. A problem of relations between absolutely and relatively privileged and absolutely and relatively deprived is projected as a special, detachable problem of relations between coloured and white. There is then it is true a 'radical' consciousness of 'race', both ways; a way of organizing and a way of isolating. But something that is happening as part of a system, in the world and in the society, can in these ways be specialized to an interest-group, a case on its own, an enclosed and mystifying and internally anxious area.

Managed politics uses this method, again and again: separating the issues, and moving bewilderingly from this to that. But this deep lock, of a series of limited special-interest radicalisms, is also, we must see, something we put on ourselves, in a confusing and disintegrating social transition. There are radical groupings, as we have seen, in the society, but there are also radical groupings, with the same deep problems of consciousness and connexion, inside our minds, not speaking to each other.

47. Other socialist groupings

This is also true of the more specifically socialist organizations and groupings. There are three main factors in their formation. First, reactions to the dominant record of the Labour party and its repeated political failures; second, urgent needs to find centres of socialist activity and socialist discussion, which the formal organization of the Labour party has prevented; and third, the reactions of socialists to political events elsewhere in the world. In the complication of these three factors the problems of these socialist organizations and groupings are now especially acute.

Consider first the British Communist party. It is at one level a reaction to political events elsewhere: the historic victory of the Communist party of the Soviet Union. In its origins it was a federation of a number of small Marxist and semi-Marxist groups in the years immediately following the Russian Revolution. At the same time it has always succeeded in attracting a minority of militant working-class leaders and has indeed been more successful as a militant wing of the Labour movement than as an autonomous Marxist party. Anyone who knows the British Communist party knows how much it shares in culture and outlook with the more general British working-class movement. Its strength has remained in its capacity to connect with issues directly affecting the working class, notably in industrial struggles and in tenants' organizations.

At the same time there have been deep contradictions in the party's political perspective, and these have been reflected in its internal conflicts and in the way it has been regarded by the rest of the Labour movement. Thus, from its real if limited base in authentic working-class activity, the party has seen itself as a constituent element of a wider movement, to which it should be given full access and with which, indeed, it has sought to affiliate. But then in its formal capacity as a Marxist party, and on the very basis of its militancy, it has often been forced into opposition to the official forms of the Labour movement, both industrially and politically. The uneasy co-existence of a strategy of affiliation and a strategy of opposition has not only confused the party itself: it has also led to deep suspicion of its tactics not only from the leadership but from wide areas of the membership of the Labour movement.

This contradiction has been sharpened by the difficult relation of the British Communist party to the international communist movement. Its difficult negotiation of a combined policy of affiliation and opposition has again and again been overridden, in its own actions and in the reactions of others, by events and decisions elsewhere; above all of course in the Soviet Union itself. There have been times when it has been reduced, or has reduced itself, to the role of apologist or representative of the Soviet view. On some occasions this has been justified, in periods of international reaction and crisis, but in general it has been profoundly damaging: not only because it has then had to defend actions and policies which were later changed or which were seen clearly to be indefensible; but because even when it was right, it was acquiescing in a reduction of its status from an independent party to a creature of a movement elsewhere. In recent years, following changes in the international communist movement, it has sought to regain some freedom of action in this respect, but its past lies heavily upon it in most people's eyes.

This kind of history might indeed be surpassed if the party could find a dynamic role within British history. But here again there is a contradiction. Its inherited ideology is that of revolution on the classical model; the capture of state power. Faced with the realities of a society determined by an advanced capitalism and liberal democracy, it has in practice, like other western Communist parties, modified this ideology. It sees its future in an organized popular movement and in parliamentary victories. But whereas the Communist parties of France and Italy command large working-class votes, in Britain all efforts to increase the Communist vote, even at a time of severe disillusion with a Labour government, seem to fail. In its relations with social democratic parties the British Communist party is in a unique situation, in that the Labour party is still the majority party of the British working class. The Communist party is then not a major element in any electoral federation of the Left, and the electoral strategy which it has been forced to adopt serves only to reveal its weakness.

This is not a criticism which any socialist can make complacently. It is, as we have seen, a common problem for all socialists in the present electoral system. Meanwhile, a large number of committed and active socialists have rejected the particular organization, atmosphere and methods of the Communist party, on the basis of experience. It is moreover essential for the Communist party to realize this, and not to assume that socialists will inevitably move in their direction as the Labour definition fails. The crisis of organization now posed for all socialists is unlikely to be resolved by any existing forms.

But there is a special danger for the Communist party in that it can rationalize its weakness in its own society by its formal affiliation to an immensely powerful international movement. This source of apparent comfort, which is now heavily drawn upon, is bound to be delusive. It may allow the persistence of an active minority movement with a well-organized press and with useful international connexions, but the very form of this persistence is and must be seen to be a kind of insulation. Socialists outside the Communist party have certainly the duty to resist the endemic anti-communism, the unreasoning prejudices and the actual bans and prescriptions which are used in the interest of the capitalist accommodation. But to convert this from a negative to a positive activity will require major movements and developments within the Communist party itself.

This becomes especially apparent when we look at the relations in Britain between socialist theory and political organization, and between political groupings and the course of international revolution. It is, for example, already true that many British Marxists are not and do not wish to be members of the Communist party. There are two main reasons for this. The first and least important, though it is often the easiest to describe, is the result of major splits in the international movement: as between 'Stalinism' and 'Trotskyism' in the world of the thirties and forties; and as between at one level Russia and China, and at another level orthodox and guerrilla revolutionary strategies, in the world of the sixties. Each of these major divisions has produced a fragmentation among revolutionary socialists in Britain. The resultant groups have sometimes seen themselves wholly in terms of developments elsewhere; they have become, in effect, a client Left.

More seriously, when, as has too rarely happened, such groupings have tried to become more than reflections of events elsewhere, more than the small branch offices of distant movements, and have tried to relate what they have learned to the problems of socialist activity in Britain, the extensive and destructive vocabulary of the international argument has usually been brought into play very early: to distract and displace attention and to prevent real clarification. The discovery of a relevant socialist organization in Britain, which would in any case be a difficult process, has then been overlaid by an inauthentic and superficial controversy. The international bearings of a contemporary Marxism are certainly grounds for dispute and clarification. But a premature hardening and name-calling, in which all can join, now irrationally delays an essential process, in which what has been learned from elsewhere could be significantly reapplied and relocated in the British historical situation with which it is necessary in the first instance to deal. The many kinds of effective alienation, and of rationalization of one's own predicament by attachment to other successes and predicaments, are only likely to be overcome by direct political organization and struggle in our own society. And if this is so it is essential that the secondary definitions, in terms of events elsewhere, should be overcome by primary definitions of a serious, immediate and involving strategy where we live. In this process we believe it is necessary to say that the competing orthodoxies and nominal groupings of the past will have within themselves to be overcome.

For the formation of sects by a reflection of international disputes is in fact the least important part of the contemporary evolution of socialism. The growth points now, in our view, are in the renewal of socialist activity and analysis, which of course includes the experience of revolutionary societies and movements, but which includes also the difficult response to an advanced phase of capitalism and of post-colonial imperialism. In this work the possibility of new definitions, new strategies and new organizations seems really to reside, and it would be a tragedy if this process, in which all the scattered groups of socialists might co-operate, were delayed by the priorities of received and hardened structures and commitments.

This becomes more evident when we consider the fact that perhaps the largest grouping of active socialists in Britain is now essentially unorganized. This grouping includes many who move from one temporary organization to another, and others whose only definition so far has been that they are Labour party socialists on the Labour Left. A major factor in the development of this grouping has been the complicated relation between the Labour party and other formal socialist groups. A whole dimension of international socialist thought has in effect been insulated from the independent British Left because contact with it was normally only to be attained by membership of one of the existing groups or sects. The strength of many of these Labour and independent socialists, that they were thinking continually in terms of the realities of British society, was then matched by a weakness, that in the absence of the whole socialist intellectual and political tradition they were especially vulnerable to the orthodoxies of the system they opposed.

It has been characteristic of the Labour Left, in its reaction against aspects of the international socialist movement, that it has defined itself more as a series of short-term campaigns than as a serious political strategy. In default of a theory and a strategy, it has relied excessively on passing personalities and on a consequent experience of unreasonable hopes and unexpected betrayals. In its present experience of a Labour government effectively assimilated to the new capitalism, the Labour Left reacts at first in familiar ways: tabling resolutions for the party conference; campaigning for this or that man to be elected to the National Executive Committee; calling on 'Left' ministers to be loyal to their socialism; making hopeful demands on the government for 'an immediate change of course'. All these actions are clearly based on a strategy of giving political priority to Labour in parliament, and of thinking organizationally in terms of the existing structure of the Labour party. In fact when conference resolutions are successful but are still ignored, and when what are thought of as the representatives of the Left remain part of this corrupt power, this strategy reaches or ought to reach its breaking point. At the same time, these Labour socialists, and many of the independent Left who have looked to the Labour party as the only effective political force, are extremely reluctant to move into any kind of organization which would seem to insulate them from the central areas of political decision.

It is at this point that the crucial difference we have already established, between a political movement and an electoral machine, becomes relevant. For it is certain that what has so far been thought of as the Labour Left has been a kind of shadow reproduction of the whole official Labour party and its perspectives. Just as the Labour party has been a compromise between working-class objectives and the existing power structures, at the national level, so the traditional Labour Left has been a compromise between socialist objectives and the existing power structure, at the party level. It has made important efforts to reform this party power structure, but with the odds continually against it. Alternatively it has had to choose between what are in effect electoral campaigns within the party, and political campaigns which can stand in their own right. When it chooses the electoral campaigns it becomes of necessity involved in the same kind of machine politics, the same manipulation of committee votes in the names of thousands, the same confusion of the emptying institutions of the movement with the people in whose name they are conducted, as that of the leaders and managers whom it seeks to affect or displace. It is then not only that in the game of manipulation it is always likely to lose; it is also that it is directing energy into the very machines and methods which socialists should fight.

What has happened in this evolution is a materialization of the Labour Left around certain personalities, certain M.P.s and certain short-term issues. And this has prevented the outward-looking and independent long-term campaign which would carry forward the politics of the many thousands of people who are now classified in this way. Because it is a classification rather than an organization this very large group is in effect powerless.

The Left M.P.s in parliament have made important moves and stands against right-wing policies and in that sense deserve support. It is intolerable that in their defence of an elected programme and of conference decisions they should be disciplined by the parliamentary machine, and forced to choose between an imposed 'unity' of the party and the only remaining socialist electoral identity. The critical task of the next months and years is to break the deadlock in which the Left members have found themselves, and this can be done only by extending the struggle beyond parliamentary terms, to give effect to the wishes of those thousands of independent people who are in fact the Labour Left, and who find themselves, continually, without a specific organization. This is more than a question of defending the Left members; that limited though necessary programme is within an old strategy. What has to be achieved is the autonomy of a general political campaign. The incorporation of the Labour government has forced on the whole body of the Labour Left and on other independent socialists the urgency of their own political identity and representation. In allowing their work to be dragged back, constantly, to the needs of a general electoral campaign, or of a subsidiary electoral campaign within the Labour party, they are failing to establish what they are clearly strong enough to establish: a political campaign that could operate, without conventional restrictions, in the society as a whole.

48. The unions and politics

In the trade union movement, socialists of all shades of opinion in fact work together. The political range of an undivided movement is still very important. It of course includes bitter internal struggles, but it remains an outstanding and characteristic achievement of the British working class. The relation between this undivided movement and the political structure of the Left has been, throughout, the key issue of socialist politics. In the transitional character of the current social crisis, this issue is posed again in a very sharp and complicated form.

We have seen that it is an essential part of the strategy of new capitalist politics to incorporate the trade unions in its own kind of central institutions. In effect, an offer is made, under the apparently progressive slogans of 'national planning' and 'responsible co-operation', which can to some extent coincide with the views of many trade unionists on recognition of the rights of labour, and on replacing economic anarchy with a new kind of co-operative order. With this offer, certain tangible benefits can also be proposed: a planned growth of production, security of employment, rational relations between wages and prices: all policies which concern trade unions in a central way. It is then not surprising that the offer has, to a considerable extent, been accepted; but of course this is not just a model situation, it is a real economy. In practice, not only have these precise benefits failed to materialize (which might only mean that we should try harder along the same lines), but also the unions have found themselves having to operate, increasingly, within a definition of the economic crisis which puts the major responsibility for causing it and curing it on them.

We have already exposed this false definition, but the way in which the corporate institutions were set up, the terms in which the offer was made and accepted, make a change of course very difficult. Involved in machinery which seemed sensible and progressive, the unions have at the same time to take the full weight of a planned propaganda operation against them. Strikes, which by comparison with other advanced industrial countries are at a comparatively low figure in Britain, are ruthlessly used to raise prejudice against trade unionists; moreover, as in the case of the seamen, the dockers and the railwaymen, an industrial dispute is now quickly escalated, within a prepared political context, to the level of confrontation with the State and with the national economy. The central importance of everything that the working class does, in the actual running of the country, is now only ever raised in this negative way: when they temporarily stop doing it, or when they ask, as the price of doing it, for fair wages and conditions.

But though the members of an individual union in dispute defend their position with stubborn good sense, a total defence, and its corresponding claims, are hardly ever made with the necessary combined strength. As a movement, though not, fortunately, in their particular capacities, the unions have been made guilty and politically defensive about the forms of a capitalist crisis, and can, at times, be persuaded that it is by their sacrifice that it must be solved.

We have seen the policies that would be necessary to solve the crisis in a different way, compatible with the interests of the millions of ordinary people whom the trade unions represent. But the politics of this solution, as it directly concerns the trade union movement, are especially difficult. It is true that the unions can never be incorporated into new capitalism as completely as, say, the Labour party: they are under too regular and too intense pressures from their members. But this can lead to major internal problems, of which the signs are already very clear. When the Tories talk about a strong trade union movement, they mean one in which the national officers would have firm control over their members. Yet in any organization as difficult as a trade union, the need for strong central control, to enforce the ethic of collective action, is also, to some extent, authentic. This fact has to be set beside the inevitable occurrence, in any leadership which has had to exist for a long time in the forms of capitalist society, of careerism, authoritarianism, and bureaucracy.

The necessary political point is then very difficult to make. Socialists must obviously support the local militant leaders who do so much actual union work and who confront the real pressures of capitalist society not indirectly and on paper but in day-to-day experience. We must also support the struggles for internal union democracy which are so clearly necessary, against actual authoritarian and bureaucratic structures and against forms of organization which, offering certain finite benefits (at about the level of insurance) to union members, do no more than this, on behalf of their members, but act in effect as organizing and disciplining agents of employers and of the State. This is precisely the role which is proposed to the whole union movement, by new capitalism, in return for limited economic benefits. And because this is so, socialists must inevitably be at the side of those fighting to maintain an active and democratic movement which is unambiguously on the wage earner's side.

But all real institutions take time to build, and agitational work in the unions, which is critical if their real functions are to be maintained and extended, must not be confused with what looks like an attractive short cut, with industrial militancy bypassing the unions, only to find itself then faced with the full power of the capitalist state. The situation is so bad, in some industries and unions, that this latter course is often inevitable, but as a general strategy the alternative course, in which the unions are made more militant by being made more democratic, and more democratic by the continual fact of militancy, is obviously stronger.

Another way of making this same point is to consider again the famous formulation of the 'limitations of trade union consciousness'. Trade unions, it is said, forced to play the market within market terms, take on the character of institutions operating within capitalism: in some opposition of course, but limited by that perspective; and then changing, in themselves, to capitalist forms of organization and consciousness. Some part of this is true, in regular experience. But in the very carrying out of their functions, under either economic or more general democratic pressures from their members, trade unions reach the point of incompatibility with capitalism, and especially with a secondary capitalism, again and again. The new capitalist model, so apparently accepted only two years ago, has collapsed in unemployment and wage restraint. The disappointment of most trade union leaders is then obvious. But just because that political role was thrust on the trade union movement, to complete the structures of new capitalist politics, it is not only in local struggles that the eventual incompatibility is demonstrated; it is also nationally, and in the most public way.

Without unofficial strikes, there would now be very little active resistance to the new capitalist state. In that sense, they are at the heart of the democratic struggle. But they are only at the heart of the socialist struggle if they are taken beyond their inevitably local and particularized issues, to the point where trade union consciousness ends and political consciousness begins. And the means to this is the organized national movement, which, as in the Trades Union Congress of 1967, represents, in its major policies, the most formidable political challenge the present system now faces. Most of the signs are that this will continue to be true, and it is especially important for socialists, involved they must be with local democracy and local militancy, to understand and connect with the significance of this national development.

British trade unions passed the limits of trade union consciousness, and entered political consciousness, in the early years of this century when, under threat of the use of law against them, they created the Labour party. Much can be said about their failure to develop this political creation, in their own interests; indeed while they were talking, as trade unionists often bitterly do, about socialist intellectuals, they had their party effectively taken off them by non-socialist intellectuals, to the point where in an economic crisis it could be turned directly back against them. That real history has still to be remembered and understood.

But the character of the present crisis, as we have argued throughout, is transitional, and in nothing more so than this. The undivided industrial movement, the organized working-class coalition, created a party in its own image, which was also thought of as a coalition. Under the pressure of crisis, the internal development of the Labour party, which had been masked for so long, is now in the open for everyone to see. Familiar forms will not be given up, or even changed, without great reluctance. The weight of inertia, and the sheer intricacy of change, are also delaying factors. But the trade union movement now faces again, in a severe form, the threat of restrictive and damaging legislation. It can resist this, in limited ways, by industrial action, but as a whole it is going to be a political battle: perhaps the most decisive, in Britain, in this decade. If the legislation is actually proposed by a Labour government, the crisis will be unusually open. If it is delayed till the Tories, the internal effects on the Labour party will still be acute. And in this battle - faced by concentrated propaganda, by areas of public opinion led into hostility to the unions, by the facts of state power, and by the contradictions of their own degree of direct incorporation and the more settled incorporation of the official Labour party - the trade unions will not have much choice: it will be political change, or it will be serious and lasting defeat.

In preparation for this decisive struggle, co-operation between socialists in and outside the trade unions is urgently necessary. Much of the necessary battle, in matters of law and ideology, will have to be fought quite generally, by socialists with the necessary professional skills. The essential strategy will be determined by the unions themselves, but socialists in and outside the unions have the duty to indicate its political perspectives. For what has been a passive contradiction in British society, between an organized working class and its political party steadily converting to capitalism, seems certain to become, under the pressures of economic crisis, active and even dynamic. The central strength of the Left in Britain, in the organized working class, has been for a long time locked in apparently immovable political difficulties. There will be no simple liberation now, but the politics of trade unionism is again precarious, active and open, and as such can be made decisive in the general development of the Left.

49. The bearings of change

When a social system is changing, it is not only the directing institutions which change with it; it is also the institutions of opposition and protest. This can be understood in two ways: as the incorporation of previous opposition institutions - in our own time, the pressure on the Labour party, and, through it, on the unions, to accept the procedures of new capitalism - but also as the emergence of different kinds of opposition responding in a new language and with new kinds of organization to tensions and deprivations that are felt in new ways.

We believe it follows from our main analysis of the present crisis, and of the particular strategies that have been selected to overcome it, that British political institutions are now entering a period of profound strain, in just such a time of transition. We have described and attacked the ruling strategies, and we believe that they are in fact very widely opposed. But it is then characteristic, of the kind of change we are describing, that the organization of this widespread opposition faces its own severe problems. Our point in describing the difficulties, the limitations and the contradictions of existing kinds of organized opposition was not to try to establish some position of superiority, from which a single new answer would be handed down. On the contrary, in describing the difficulties of socialist working-class and radical organizations, we were describing our own situation, and at many points criticizing ourselves.

And because this is so, we can share, very readily, one initial reaction: that to describe the situation as it is can be demoralizing; that it can take toll of an energy which is already in many cases at full stretch. Nothing would have been easier, in one way, than to beat the drum, to make the equivalent of a conference speech, to state and imply that victory is quite near, if this or that can be done. Our decision not to do this was not a reluctance for that kind of excitement, though it has to be said that the rhetoric which has poured from the Left, in the last twenty years - matching in kind and style the perpetual exhortations of the career politicians - can be very damaging: rousing, in unreasoning ways, energies that are only too willingly given and that can only too easily be exhausted, in yet another false dawn. We know too well the men and women who have lived in these ways, and have at last, utterly tired, pulled back to make other decisions and other settlements.

To fail to recognize this mood is to miss an essential element of the present crisis of opposition. But then it was not only a matter of intellectual honesty, and of respect for the real experience of ourselves and others, that prompted our decision to describe this crisis in its real terms. It was also that the central finding of our analysis seemed to us to be that the crisis of the Left is precisely related to the transitional crises of new capitalism and imperialism. To describe those systems was a way of gaining consciousness, but it was a way of seeing, also, many of the sources of our own problems. What we have now to say, about a positive socialist response, is not an exhorting addendum; it is the working through of that same description and analysis.

Take first what seems now to many socialists the critical choice: whether to go on working in established Left institutions, even though they have been incorporated and diluted; or to make the break to a new organization and campaign. This is, precisely, a problem of a transitional period. The struggle against incorporation is in fact inevitable: as in the case of the trade unions, anything that has been won can, in this period, be lost, whether it is full employment or hard-won trade union rights. To fail to join in that critical struggle would be a total abdication of responsibility. It is in this sense, too, that the struggle in the Labour party is still important, because although its political incorporation has gone very far, and its conversion to machine politics continually frustrates democratic initiatives, it rests still on a contradiction: that it is the party created and financed by the organized working class, and that unless the incorporation of the trade unions is successful, its terms of conversion are extremely precarious.

What might then be concluded is that defence of the existing organizations is the first priority: a kind of last-ditch stand. But we believe it also follows from our analysis that this is a prescription for defeat. For in any rapidly evolving situation, and given the powers of the new capitalism to manage political crises and to build public opinion, any simple defensive strategy is quite quickly isolated and penetrable. Victory, in such a struggle, would be at most the scaling-down of some outrageous demand, and the terms of this would be the acceptance of some more apparently modest demand. We have already seen this in the case of an 'incomes policy'. For the means of incorporation, in the managed politics we now have, is just this incremental process: what can look, from outside, like a drift, but is in fact a piecemeal development of a clear overall intention.

What we are always in danger of forgetting - as in the case of incomes policy, or of escalation of the war in Vietnam - is that the forces we oppose are by their very nature not static, and so cannot be met by any simple fixed defence. Capitalism is in one sense the permanent revolution: endlessly restless and active in the pursuit of profit and the protection of the conditions of profit. Imperialism, in our own time, is not, though it may sometimes appear to be, a counter-revolution; it is an active, flexible strategy for control of the world. Against forces as inventive, as developing, and as powerful as these, existing positions can only be defended by active struggle: not by digging in on the *status quo*, but by making new demands, and continually raising the terms of the conflict. Otherwise, what looked like a confrontation turns out to have been a bargain; changes *of* the system reappear as changes *in* the system; and the lines of defence are continually weakened.

We have already said that the unions can only successfully defend their present legal rights by a campaign which, disclosing the realities of capitalist economic power and decision-making, discloses in those facts the substantial and growing needs of organized labour, as a human claim rather than a traditional apology. Similarly, in the Labour party, there is nothing to go back to, whether it is the words of Clause Four or a primitive party democracy. The demands that have to be made are in terms of the need for a contemporary political movement, capable of opposing the new capitalism. The shell of an old movement has been occupied by the body of a new; it is not by defending the shell, but by making and pressing an alternative body of policies and demands, that anything can be saved.

There is then no necessary contradiction between the defence of existing organizations and the development of new ones. Unless new organizations of demand and protest are powerfully developed, the old ones will in any case wither away. But it is again clear from our analysis that a discontinuity, between new and old kinds of demands, and between the areas of new demands themselves, is not accidental, but is a precise consequence of the character of the ruling system. Its whole tactic is to incorporate a form of the existing demands, at the point where they threaten the operation of the system, and then to prevent, elsewhere, the making of new connexions. In reality, of course, the connexions are in any case difficult. The problems of poverty and homelessness in Britain, of racial discrimination, of low wages, of militarism, of the control of communications, of war, disturbance and hunger in the poor two thirds of the world, come through discontinuously, and we can find ourselves moving our attention from this to that, in a desperate competition of priorities set against limited resources and time. Here again, the reason for the fragmentation, the discontinuity, of Left and radical opinion, is a characteristic of the system as it is experienced. The facts, in the end, cannot really be hidden, and when they are out, people respond to them. This is the social reality of the period of single-issue campaigns. Everything is then done to interpret each particular cruelty or deprivation as a special claim on our conscience, which in its urgency is wholly preoccupying. What is not normally done is to connect the issues, and to follow them through to a political and economic system.

We have had close experience of the different single-issue campaigns. We know the dedication and energy that is given to them. But there can be also a corresponding impatience with other kinds of demand: 'let us at least deal with this'. It was from just this experience, in repeated campaigns, that we set out on this Manifesto. And what we have learned, in the course of following the issues through from our different initial priorities, is that a new total description, however preliminary, is now indispensable. Against the inherent power and speed of the system we oppose, only a whole position can effectively stand.

This is then our own immediate political decision: that the first thing to do, against a discontinuous experience, is to make and insist on connexions: a break and development in consciousness, before we can solve the problems of organization. It is easy to dismiss this effort as merely intellectual work: a substitution of thought for action. Our orthodox culture continually prompts this response: 'action not words' are the first obligatory words, from many apparently different men. But we reject this separation of thought and action, or of language and reality. If you are conscious in certain ways, you will act in certain ways, and where you are not conscious you will fail to act. It is not, of course, enough to describe and analyse a particular crisis; but unless socialists do it, other descriptions and analyses take over, and the best life of the society is pushed back to its margins, its gaps, its precarious unwritten areas. When we first asked ourselves the question - what action can we take? - our answer was to try to establish this practical opposition: an alternative view of our world. The organization we evolved, not without difficulty, was to reach that goal.

But it is then of course apparent, especially to us, that describing the connexions, of the system we oppose, is not making the connexions, of the life and activity we support. What we finally identify are the reasons for the existing incorporation and discontinuity. But what we began by knowing is that, through and in spite of these, an unprecedented number of people, in many different ways, are opposing this system. It is not for us as a separate group, but for all the people now in various kinds of opposition, to consider the practical problems of connexion. The bearing of what we have done is to try to initiate a process which, if successful, would go far beyond ourselves, though we should still belong to it. It is in this spirit, and on the basis of the kind of analysis this has been, that we present our practical organizational suggestions.

50. The politics of the manifesto

We propose, first, certain specific work, which we are qualified to do, in co-operation with trade unions and other organizations of the Labour movement, and with some of the major campaigns. Research and publication, in direct relation to particular struggles, and a more continuing educational activity, are now urgently needed. We believe, as we have indicated, that the Left must develop its own Socialist National Plan, moving from an increasing solidity of defence to detailed developments and proposals. Our own resources, at the present stage, are limited, but there is a potential for rapid growth if the channels of this co-operation can be established.

It is in activity, and not by some central or sudden organizational decision, that a new Left will come into being. In this transitional period, what is done will be more important than what it is called. We call our own manifesto 'May Day', because that is where we can all start.

On some issues, notably in the peace movement, the Left in the sixties has shown the will and the capacity to work together. But the form of this unity, as on the Aldermaston marches, carries an important lesson. Many groups and individuals worked together, but in their own right and in their own identity. This is especially the mood of the new young Left of the sixties. Association and co-operation have to be open and equal. Nobody, faced with these actual people, can narrow his eyes and calculate; count recruits and a rank-and-file. Or rather, anybody can do this, but he will get nowhere; the mood to co-operate is not in that style. And in this the young of the sixties are joined by many of their predecessors: willing, in the right cause, to give their energy, but not to be used, recruited, hardened or matured by any political calculator. There will be maturing and hardening, as already in demonstrations and other co-operative work. But we shall all be moving, all deciding: the institutions we want prefigured in the institutions we create to fight for them; or we shall not be there at all.

This in itself rules out, and for good reasons, any simple idea of a centralizing new Left. But of course it does not rule out, indeed it indicates, particular and contemporary forms of co-operation and unity. It is already necessary to improve the exchange of information, between different groups on the Left, and between different countries: not only on dates and meetings, though these are important; but on plans of future activities, on research and discussion in progress, on the lessons of particular types of activity. We think such an information service might be begun almost immediately. It will also be necessary, in our view, to begin work on a directory of Left and radical organizations: both as a way of mapping the ground and to put people in touch with each other. Such a directory would need, in practice, to be organized both by localities and by interests.

These functions extend to the situation of the Left press. The *Morning Star* and *Tribune* are now both in danger; the *Sunday Citizen* is dead. There are immediate problems here, in that the surviving papers represent particular viewpoints with which we may only in part agree. But we believe this will be an early test of the seriousness of the Left: to save these papers, from what would be their suppression by capitalism, and to go on from that to co-operate in circulating and publicizing the many other Left papers and magazines - the *Voice* papers, *Peace News*, *International Socialism*, *New Left Review* and others - which are now an active socialist and radical culture. It would of course be economically easier if these papers were closer to each other, or even in some cases merged. But our original principle operates here: it is very important that groups retain their own identity, while they feel it to be necessary; even that groups should see their own papers as in argument and contention with others on the Left, in the necessary process of discussion and dispute; but still, recognizing an effective community against a system which suppresses or reduces them, that they should help each other, in practical and immediate ways, so that the socialist and radical culture stays active and can extend.

It is natural, given the emphasis of the Manifesto on the crucial need to connect and communicate, that we should consider first these connecting functions. An information service, a directory and an extending press would operate first, mainly, on a national and international level. Yet similar co-operation is no less necessary, and is indeed often easier, in our actual communities.

We have had some experience, since our original Manifesto, of the formation of local groups of new kinds. In the most successful cases, groups have been formed which contain, for the first time for very many years, members of all the different areas of the socialist, working-class and radical movements. Simply to get in one room, and agreeing to meet again, Labour councillors and party members, C.N.D. activists, trade union officials and members, Communist party members, and representatives of the many groupings on the independent Left is a real achievement. It has been done, and is still happening. At best there are tensions, and some necessary disagreements. At worst, there have been attempts to steer the group to some more specific affiliation, and it has then in some cases broken up. We are collecting and analysing these different experiences, so that we can go on working and trying.

Where such a local group has been successful, it has very soon liberated energies, begun new educational and campaigning work, and, crucially, contributed to an understanding of a new situation in which most of us are moving and are prepared to move. Such a group, ideally, should be autonomous. It should not require of its members that they give up their existing affiliations and identities. This is possible in towns and in educational institutions where political activity is already strong. But there have been other cases, when a group has formed directly in response to the Manifesto, with no prior or binding affiliations elsewhere. We welcome this, and try to keep in touch through an organizer and a bulletin. But it follows from our whole analysis and approach that we do not want to set up the kind of centralizing organization which would demand any premature decision of loyalties. We are interested in promoting a connecting process, in what we see as a transitional period, in response to the Manifesto as an argument. Where it is the only means of organization, we accept that responsibility, but where it is a connecting process, between existing organizations, to which members still give their loyalties, we are also satisfied. We have in fact been overwhelmed by letters and requests for speakers; we are re-organizing to cope with them. But while we do all that necessary organizational work, we wish to continue to make clear that what we are offering to the Left is connected discussion and connected activity around an analysis of the crisis; to start there, and to see where we go. We are not, that is to say, trying to make any kind of take-over bid; the situation is too serious and too complicated for that.

Much of the important work, on and around the Manifesto, will go on in local groups, of the kinds described, and in special-interest groups, which we intend to actively promote. The intellectual organization, to produce the Manifesto, was of course improvised; but in bringing together working groups, from economists to teachers, it made an interesting and significant advance. We shall build on this, and are now looking into the form of a permanent organization of this kind.

Immediate work and continuing work. Given the scale of the crisis, some of these crucial informing and connecting processes seem limited, though it is in these ways, always, that a serious movement is conceived. As we move into longer perspectives, which of course begin today and where we are, we see certain crucial tasks. There are the many specific campaigns we shall have in any case to work in: as allies, in an active presence, against imperialism, in the peace movement, in industrial disputes and wages struggles, in defence of the trade unions, in rent cases, in community developments. At most points, there, we shall be working with thousands of others, and are glad to do so. In some cases, especially in community work, we are joining with others in initiating particular projects. But in most of this active campaigning we join with, indeed now belong to, an already structured Left. We intend to take our share of the ordinary duties, but what, specifically, we bring to these movements is a developed analysis: of course for discussion, for amendment, for further development.

We believe it is possible, though we would not make the claim arrogantly, that the Manifesto analysis, which is more important than any separate Manifesto group, could act as a catalyst, in this difficult transition, to build a new Left. We do not come to this cut-and-dried; but we come with urgency, with conviction, and with a determination hardened in the very exploration of the system we confront. This, in our view, is an absolute commitment, for, faced by that system, we are bound to withdraw our allegiance from it and from all its instruments. We resume our own initiatives, by a sense of absolute need. The major division in contemporary British politics is between acceptance and rejection of the new capitalism and imperialism: its priorities, its methods, its versions of man and of the future. The most urgent political need in Britain is to make this basic line evident, and to begin the long process of unambiguous struggle and argument at this decisive point. We intend, therefore, to draw this political line, at any time, where it actually is, rather than where it might be thought convenient for elections or traditional descriptions. What we constitute, by this Manifesto, is just this kind of conscious presence and opposition: intellectual, in this first instance, but also wherever that may lead.

We reject, therefore, consensus politics, but that necessary hardening must go along with a new flexibility, where the real opposition is already formed and forming. We look forward to making certain specific connexions, in campaigns and in publications. We want to ask members of the major single-issue campaigns and of the existing organizations of the Labour movement to discuss with us and others the bearings of their own urgent work on the whole analysis we have offered, and its corresponding bearings on them. We want to make this specific, wherever possible: as between the problem of poverty and the demand for a minimum wage, which are deeply connected issues but which are dealt with, now, in quite different kinds of organization; as on technological change, areas of high unemployment and declining industries, and the many consequent problems of community movement and community redevelopment, which are now being discussed in separate groups and contexts; as on relations between the United States and Europe, including the relations between Britain and Europe, bringing groups together from different countries; as on world hunger and poverty in direct relation to technical problems of aid and trade, where again the groups are now normally different; as on the relations between education and industrial training, where a class division is now built in; as on the relations between racial inequality, deprived communities and deprived countries, which are now in different dimensions; as on nuclear disarmament and the problems of armed revolution, in the Third

World, where instincts, loyalties and organizations can conflict; as on artists and routinized schools, where a particular bringing together, exploring what is meant by education and personal development, could bring important results; as on low wages and high military spending, the political alliance and the techniques of the monetary system, managed politics and voluntary politics. None of this work will be easy, but we see it as an extension from print, where we have connected these issues, to people and organizations who are directly concerned with them. In the process of such work, which is of course notably worth doing for its own sake, we shall be looking, openly, for any possibility of active co-operation which might lead beyond the specific project. In the same spirit, we shall invite existing socialist and radical organizations and groupings to join in this work, and to go on learning from each other and from others.

This is a serious programme, but we shall only be satisfied when a Left has been built that is at once contemporary in experience, educated in method, democratic in organization, and strong in action. We have not tried to predict the immediate future. In certain ways, the middle ground of politics is being broken down, as the whole crisis deepens. But we are assuming that this middle ground has a considerable capacity to reconstitute itself, under new names and forms. And we are sufficiently close to British experience to know how tenaciously, and how understandably, a sharpening of conflict is avoided, or goes on being blurred. But we have tried to take the measure of a world crisis, and of Britain inextricably caught up in it, and we believe that no conflict is now too sharp, and that political decision has never been more serious.

We want then to connect with what is still strong in Britain: a democratic practice, a determined humanity, an active critical intelligence. We want to connect with these forces in our country, which are our own sources and resources, so that we can co-operate in deep social changes and in new relationships with the rest of the world. The years immediately ahead will be confusing and testing, but we believe that by making a position clear now, we can play an effective part in a necessary realignment and redirection of British politics. What we are seeking to define is an active socialism of the immediately coming generation: an emerging political process rather than the formalities of a process that is already, as democratic practice, beginning to break up and disappear. We are looking to the political structure of the rest of the century, rather than to the forms which now embody the past and confuse recognition of the present.

This manifesto is a challenge and it asks for a response. There are thousands who share our intentions and our values, and who can connect with and contribute to our analysis and our future work.

Those who stand in our situation: we invite your active support.